35 HIKING TRAILS
COLUMBIA RIVER GORGE

BY DON & ROBERTA LOWE

The Touchstone Press
P.O. Box 81
Beaverton, Oregon 97075

I.S.B.N. 0-911518-61-4
Copyright © 1980
by Don and Roberta Lowe

Maps Courtesy of
U.S. Geological Survey

INTRODUCTION

The approximately 170 miles of trails in the Columbia Gorge, most within an hour's drive of Portland, provide some of the best hiking in the Northwest. This region of uncounted waterfalls, steep-sided canyons and lush vegetation is a remarkable place. Every portion of every route is scenic (no slogs through mediocre woods just to reach one viewpoint here); the trails range from short, almost level strolls to complex, strenuous loops that can take one or more full days; and many of these superb routes are open all year with each season having its special allure — the wildflowers of spring, the softness of summer, the varied hues of autumn and the starkness of winter.

Geomorphologically, the Columbia River Gorge extends east from Troutdale for 55 miles to The Dalles but, to most people, "the Gorge" means that stretch of sheer-walled, wooded slopes from Crown Point to Hood River on the Oregon side. This impressive area is the result of successive layers of basalt flows, mudflows and other volcanic debris that have been eroded by the Columbia River. The first deposit was the Ohanapecosh Formation laid down in the Upper Eocene Era. This rock is rich in a clay that becomes slippery when wet, thus promoting landslides, and tilts 2° to 10° toward the river on the Washington side. This feature accounts, in part, for the less spectacular nature of the north slope. The earliest rock that can be seen today, however, is of the Eagle Creek Formation laid down during the Upper Eocene. The next major deposit has been identified as Yakima basalt. At the base of Elowah Falls (No. 16) you can see a 250-foot high layer of the Eagle Creek Formation topped by a layer of Yakima basalt. The south face of Hamilton Mountain (No. 1) has eroded and slipped away to reveal a canyon that was cut into the Eagle Creek Formation and subsequently filled by a flow of Yakima basalt. In addition to stream deposition and other accumulations during the Plio-Pleistocene, wide-spread volcanism occurred, resulting in such landmarks as Larch Mountain (No's. 9, 10 and 12). Olivine basalt flows continued into the early Pleistocene-Holocene. Mt. Defiance (No. 33) was formed during this period and the Indian legend of the Bridge of the Gods, possibly the result of a massive landslide, may have begun then. The eras of build-up have ceased in the Gorge and now the forces of erosion are wearing them down again. Usually, this is a protracted process but looking at the immense slippage from Table Mountain and the considerably smaller, but still impressive, slide along Tanner Creek (No. 18) graphically illustrates that some major changes can happen quickly.

When the first white men passed through the Gorge, the Indians had been there for a considerable length of time — all those legends about the fiery goings-on between Wy'east (Mt. Hood) and Pa-toe (Mt. Adams) certainly must have been based on some rather impressive volcanic activity. Probably the first white men to be in the vicinity of the Gorge were Lt. Broughton of the British Royal Navy and his crew who in 1792 sailed up the Columbia River as far as the Sandy River. The first documented persons who actually traversed the length of the Gorge were members of the Lewis and Clark Expedition in 1805. After spending an exceedingly wet winter on the northern Oregon coast, they retraced their route up the Columbia River the following spring. In 1810 David Thompson of the Canadian Northwest Company, a fur trading firm, came down the river and camped at the present site of Cascade Locks. He, too, returned upstream the following year. In 1823 David Douglas, the famed botonist, explored the area behind Beacon Rock.

Until the late 1840's when the Barlow Road was developed over the southern slope of Mt. Hood, all settlers heading west from The Dalles to the Willamette Valley had to float themselves and their belongings down the Columbia River on bateaux, a not entirely safe method of transport given the then untamed nature of the river. At that time only a faint path, seldom used even by the Indians, provided a land route through the Gorge. But beginning in the 1840's better ways of passage were developed. In 1846 Joel Palmer, for whom Palmer Peak just south of Nesmith Point (No. 15) was named, built a pack trail along the south side of the river. Understandably, portages around the rapids at the present site of Cascade Locks were a prime concern. A mule-powered flat was operated on the north side in the early 1850's and a few years later a similar system was used on the Oregon side. Steam locomotives soon replaced the animals and, in fact, the engine that Joseph Ruckel (of Ruckel Creek and Ridge, No's. 23 and 24) used on his south side portage was the first in the

Northwest. In 1855 Joseph Ruckel and a partner started the first steamship run between Portland and the Oregon portage and eventually other ships extended service to The Dalles. During the last quarter of the century, railroad service gradually was developed on the south side and the run on the north shore was inaugurated in 1908. Although many sections of road had been built by various people from the 1840's through the first decade of the 1900's, it was not until 1913 with the beginning of construction of the Columbia River Highway that the Gorge was effectively open to vehicular as well as river and rail traffic.

Not unreasonably, trail construction in the Gorge began about the same time the highway was completed. The Larch Mountain Trail (No. 9) was constructed in 1915 and the Eagle Creek Trail (No. 25) the next year by volunteer groups under the supervision of the U.S. Forest Service. The trail to Angels Rest (No. 5), then known as Fort Rock, was open as early as 1916. Over the following decades many new trails were built by Forest Service crews and volunteers. However, by the 1960's several of these routes, such as the Nesmith Point, Ruckel Creek and Herman Creek Trails (No's. 15, 23 and 28), had been abandoned and were almost impassable. But, thanks to Howard Rondthaler and other recreation-minded persons in the Forest Service (and the State Park system in the case of the upper trail to Elowah Falls, No.16) the majority of the trails that ever existed on the Oregon side of the Gorge have been reopened and even several new ones have been built.

HIKING IN THE COLUMBIA GORGE

Except for the three hikes that begin on the Washington side (No's. 1, 2 and 3), all the trips described in this guide start from, or only a short distance off, I-84, the Columbia River Highway in Oregon. (When doing the hikes in Washington you could avoid the toll on the Bridge of the Gods at Cascade Locks by taking the Interstate Bridge over the Columbia River at Portland. However, Washington 14 is no freeway and you won't save much time or gasoline.) The mileage from Portland is not given in the text when the turn-off from I-84 to the trailhead is from a numbered exit as these figures indicate the distance from that city. (i.e., the Eagle Creek Park Exit No. 41 is 41 miles east of Portland.) If you're approaching from the east and want to calculate driving mileages, the West Hood River exit is 62 miles from Portland. Not all exits from I-84 are interchanges so on some trips you'll have to continue east a short distance to the next interchange. Mention is made in the text if this will be necessary.

An especially desirable time to visit the area is during mid- to late spring. The high Cascades still are buried in snow but the Gorge is verdant with deciduous trees and colorful displays of wildflowers, particularly on open slopes such as those along the Ruckel Creek, Nick Eaton and Starvation Ridge Trails (No's 23, 27 and 34), are the equal of any alpine garden. Late fall offers crisp air and the accents of turning maple, cottonwood, oak and dogwood. Although the latter is utterly inconspicuous during the summer, its perky white blooms in spring and peach colored leaves through fall spectacularly distinguish the tree from its neighbors. The lower portions of the Gorge afford good hiking in winter when the higher routes in the Cascades are closed by snow. One bonus on these trips is sightings of many smaller waterfalls that are obscured by leafy trees during the remainder of the year. When visiting the Gorge from late fall through early spring be sure to pack extra clothing as it can be cold, wet and very windy. Paradoxically, the area can be relatively hot and humid from June through August, at least by West Coast standards.

From the Columbia River to about the 1,500 foot level the woods on the Oregon side of the Gorge are a glorious blend of deciduous and coniferous trees, vine maple, ferns, shrubs and mosses. Above this elevation the forest becomes a more simplified mix of various evergreens, including cedar, Douglas fir, hemlock and some pine. Although from west to east the woods become somewhat less lush, primarily due to the gradually decreasing rainfall, the most noticeable alteration in vegetation occurs from north to south because of the abrupt change in elevation. On any hike that has considerable climbing you will pass through several distinct zones. Besides being interesting, both visually and scientifically, meeting these bands tells you where you are along your hike. Where you spot the first clumps of beargrass you know you're around 3,000 feet and that most of your climbing is over. Considerably lower along the slopes is a narrow belt of attractive, gnarled oak that

4

you'll meet near the same elevation on several hikes. As with the geology, Washington did not fare quite as spectacularly as Oregon with its vegetation. Because of the gentler terrain, the north side was much easier to log. Also, the Yacolt Burn of 1902 devastated a considerable portion of the Washington slope. Ironically, it began near Eagle Creek but violent updrafts lifted flaming debris north across the river.

Amidst the green loveliness of the Gorge is one plant all but a few fortunate people could do without — poison oak. It is found below 1,000 feet along most of the trails but since it is reasonably low growing only your pant legs should come in contact with it and not even them if you're careful. If you're suspectible, or you live with someone who is, learn to recognize the plant, avoid touching it and after you return home shower thoroughly with a strong soap and wash your outer clothing before wearing it again.

Although bear, deer and even cougar inhabit the higher areas of the Columbia Gorge, you probably won't be fortunate enough to see them, especially if you're with other people. However, you most likely will encounter smaller animals such as squirrels, chipmunks, conies, shrews, various birds, lizards, salamanders and snakes. The only rattlesnakes you might meet on trails described in this guide would be on Dog Mountain (No. 3) from late spring through summer. Although only a few places in the Gorge are heavily infested with mosquitoes, such as sections of the Benson Plateau (No. 26), the area does have its animal equivalent to poison oak in the form of ticks. They are not at all as prevalent as the plant and they are a concern primarily in the spring. While hiking, check your and your companions' clothing frequently and at home examine your body carefully. If you find a tick using you for a lunch counter, extract it with a slow, steady pull, making sure you have removed the head and front legs. Although some people may have a red, tender spot around the bite for a few days, fortunately, to date, ticks in the northern Oregon Cascades have not carried the very serious Rocky Mountain spotted fever.

The Oregon side of the Gorge is a maze of connecting trails that is a bonanza for those who enjoy making loops. Almost every trail and possible loop in the Gorge is described, or at least mentioned, in this guide. When reference is made to another route, it is identified by its number in the book. There is no ambiguity between these numbers (1 through 35) and the ones assigned to trails by the Forest Service as the latter always have three digits, except for No. 2000, the Pacific Crest Trail. A recreation map, *Forest Trails of the Columbia Gorge*, produced in the spring of 1978 by the Mt. Hood National Forest, shows almost the entire network of routes. It can be purchased for $0.50 at the Mt. Hood National Forest headquarters, 2440 S.E. 195th, Portland, Oregon or at the Regional Office of the U.S. Forest Service, 319 S.W. Pine in downtown Portland. Although many backpacks can be made in the Gorge, its terrain and accessibility make it especially attractive for day hikes. Self-issuing backpacking permits, available at the trailhead, are required for a few routes, such as those beginning at the Columbia Gorge Work Center, and some camping restrictions exist along the heavily-used Eagle Creek Trail (No. 25).

Just as the Gorge is beautiful all year, so does it provide wonderful hiking in all kinds of weather. Woods take on a completely different character under cloud cover or when washed with rain. As you become familiar with the multi-personality of the Gorge, you'll probably find trails you actually prefer doing in the gloom. During these trips out into the infamous Oregon rain, carry a large umbrella. It will keep your head, shoulders (and glasses if you wear them) dry and you won't have to wear those ponchos that trap your body heat and get you wetter from the inside than you would from the inclement weather.

Because of the popularity of the Gorge trails, the many visitors have to be especially well-mannered if others are to enjoy their outings. Litter is amazingly scarce but if you do see some pick it up and carry it out. Orange rinds and egg shells are organic, but they decompose very slowly so don't leave them behind either. But never pick wildflowers — leave them for those who follow you to enjoy. Although potentially dangerous, the main reason why you should never cut switchbacks is that this act causes severe erosion. These proscriptions against littering, picking wildflowers and shortcutting switchbacks are familiar but, increasingly, visitors to the wilds are realizing that aural, as well as visual, pollution can detract from the enjoyment of the outdoors. Barking dogs, noisy people, radios, etc. don't belong on any trail. The Golden Rule in the outdoors is to be as inconspicuous as possible.

Except for the three hikes on the Washington side of the Gorge and No. 4 to Latourell Falls and No. 16 to Elowah Falls, all the trails in this guide are on federal land managed by the U.S. Forest Service. If you have any questions, suggestions, complaints or compliments about how the Gorge is being administered phone the Mt. Hood National Forest at 667-0511 or write to 2440 S.E. 195th, Portland 97233. For information on conservation issues contact the Oregon Environmental Council, 2637 S.W. Water Avenue, Portland 97201, telephone 222-1963. If they're not directly involved in the particular issue that concerns you, they'll refer you to a group that is. Comments intended for the authors can be sent to them in care of The Touchstone Press, P.O. Box 81, Beaverton, Oregon 97075.

Good Hiking!

D.L.
R.L.

area map - *shaded areas covered by large maps, pages 8-9*

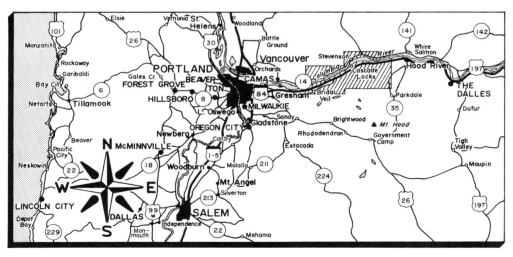

contents

LEGEND

⬡	Starting Point
- - - -	Trail
....	Obscure Trail
△	Campsite
▲	Campground
◼◣	Building or Remains
4.0	Mileage
No.79	Trail No.
S-32	Road No.
⌒━	Bridge
= = =	Secondary Road
▬▬	Primary Road

west section

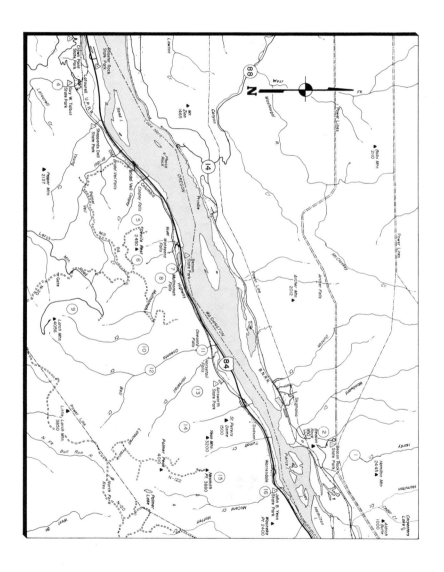

east section

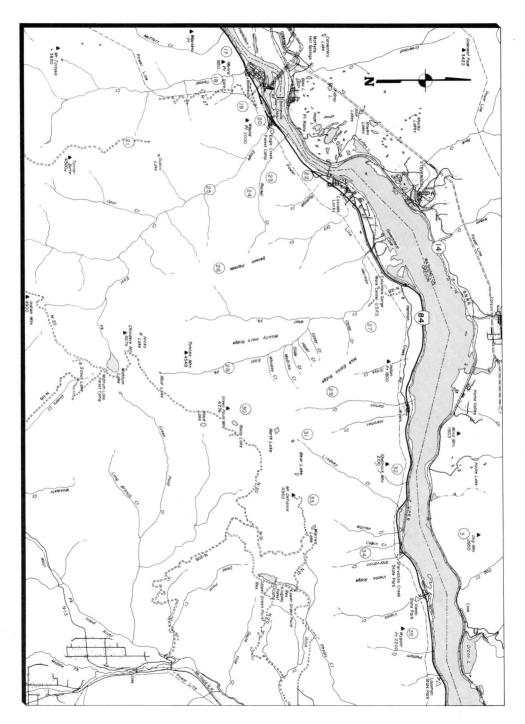

1 HAMILTON MOUNTAIN

One day trip
Distance: 3.5 miles one way (shorter route):
          8 miles as a loop
Elevation gain: 2,100 feet
High point: 2,445 feet
Allow 2 hours one way
Usually open March through November
Topographic map:
   U.S.G.S. Bridal Veil, Wash.-Oreg.
   15'   1954

Although a popular hike during the nine months it is open, the climb of Hamilton Mountain, like the trip up Dog Mountain (No. 3), is especially suitable in late fall and early spring when many of the trails on the Oregon side of the Gorge still are closed by snow or are in perpetual shade. Late in 1976 a trail was completed that makes a loop possible along the upper two thirds of the trek. The contrast in terrain and vegetation between the eastern and western portions of the circuit is remarkable.

Drive on Washington 14 seven miles west of the Bridge of the Gods or 34.5 miles east of Vancouver and across from Beacon Rock turn north onto a road identified by a sign pointing to State Park. A short, spectacular trail winds up from the south side of the highway to the top of Beacon Rock (No. 2), the plug of an eroded volcano. Follow the spur road north for 0.6 mile up to the large parking lot for the picnic area. The Hamilton Mountain Trail begins just north of the rest rooms at a large wooden sign.

Climb along mostly open slopes then pass under power lines, keeping right on the main trail where two paths go left. The second (higher) trail goes to a campground above the picnic area. Enter woods and traverse gradually up the west side of a large basin. Occasionally, you can glimpse your destination beyond the curtain of tree limbs.

Drop slightly, cross two foot bridges and keep left where a side path descends for about 100 feet to a view of Hardy Creek. Cross a side stream, the last dependable, easily accessible source of water, and traverse in several short ups and downs to the junction of a short spur that goes left to Pool of the Winds, a rock-walled chamber at Rodney Falls. The main trail switchbacks down to the bridge at the base of the falls, one of the most attractive in the Columbia Gorge. Wind up in two short switchbacks to a junction. The spur on the right descends for 100 yards, losing 75 feet of elevation, to stream level at the top of Hardy Falls. The main trail climbs in six switchbacks to a fork, the lower end of the possible loop trip.

If you decide to follow the newer route, 1.5 miles longer but with a gentler grade, keep left and traverse gradually up along the forested slope. Eventually, leave the lushness usually associated with this section of the Gorge and enter a region of deciduous growth. This area and the slopes to the west and north were devastated during the Yacolt Burn of 1902. Meet a road, turn right then after 200 yards come to a fork and keep right again. Continue following the road up to a ridge crest where you will have views of Table, Wind and Dog Mountains, Beacon Rock, the Columbia River and Mt. Hood. Walk south cross-country along the ridge crest to an outcropping and veer right (west). The trail tread resumes and traverses along the west side of the slope, dropping slightly a few times. Begin a moderately steep climb, switchback left, then turn right at a crest and travel at a more gradual grade along the narrow ridge top to the junction with the eastern half of the loop. To reach the summit viewpoint, keep left and walk several yards to a flat spot surrounded by brush.

If you choose to follow the older route on the way up, keep right at the junction at 1.6 miles. Make a score of mostly short switchbacks through woods to an area of cliffs, a good choice for a lunch stop when the summit is windy. Keep left where a side path goes to a viewpoint and traverse along the northwest side of the cliff area then climb an open, rocky face in many very short switchbacks. Travel in several longer ones up a sparsely-wooded slope, turn right at the junction of the westerly portion of the loop and come to the summit where you can see, among other landmarks, Mounts Hood, Adams and St. Helens and Bonneville Dam.

Bridge over Hardy Creek

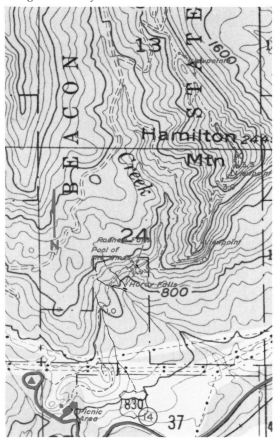

2 BEACON ROCK and NATURE TRAIL

One-half day trip
Distance: Beacon Rock, 0.8 mile one way
          Nature Trail, 0.7 mile one way
Elevation gain: Beacon Rock, 600 feet
               Nature Trail, 150 feet;
                    loss 150 feet
High Point: 850 feet
Allow ½ hour one way for Beacon Rock;
    45 minutes for Nature Trail Loop
Usually open all year (except during periods of
    severe winter weather)
Topographic map:
    U.S.G.S. Bridal Veil, Wash.-Oreg.
    15'   **1954**

Beacon Rock, that sheer faced monolith rising 850 feet above the Columbia River a short distance west of Bonneville Dam, is one of the most impressive and easily identified landmarks in the Gorge. The rock was purchased in 1915 by Henry Biddle and that year he began constructing a trail to the top. The task was completed in the surprisingly short span of three years. Although climbing routes on Beacon Rock tax even the most skilled, this trail is moderately graded and safe, what with the catwalks and guard rails.

Since the winding ascent is short, you easily can combine the climb with the loop along the recently completed Nature Trail at the southwestern base of the rock that winds through woods and circles a small lake. Energetic types could combine these two easy trips with the climb of nearby Hamilton Mountain (No. 1).

Proceed on Washington 14 to a point 34.5 miles east of the Interstate Bridge between Portland and Vancouver or 7.0 miles west of the Bridge of the Gods to a parking area off the south shoulder in front of a building with restrooms or the turnout a few hundred feet to the west along the highway at the start of the Nature Trail.

To make the climb of Beacon Rock, walk a few hundred feet either west along the highway shoulder from the paved parking area or east from the beginning of the Nature Trail to the large sign identifying the beginning of the route up Beacon Rock. Climb briefly, head south and east for a short distance to the base of the rock and then begin the steady, zigzag climb to the summit.

Understandably, the view from the top is extensive and engrossing. The peak with cliffs forming its southern face above to the northeast is Hamilton Mountain and the highpoint directly across the river on the Oregon side is Nesmith Point (No. 15).

Before you follow the Nature Trail, read the information on the bulletin board to whet your appetite for some of the animals you might be fortunate enough to see on the loop. Climb and then descend along steps. Continue gradually downhill through more open terrain and then drop, again on steps, to the northwest end of the lake and the junction of the trail that circles the shore.

To make the loop, go to the junction at the northeast end of the lake and climb steeply to an old road bed. To reach a viewpoint, turn right and walk several yards to the east. To complete the loop, turn left (west) and travel a few yards to the junction with the trail you followed in. Turn sharply right — don't follow the path that heads north — and retrace your route.

Beacon Rock from the air

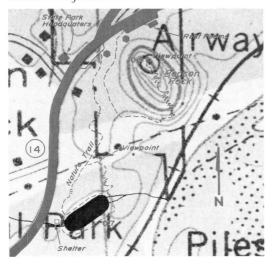

13

3 DOG MOUNTAIN

One day trip
Distance: 3.5 miles one way
Elevation gain: 2,900 feet
High Point: 3,000 feet
Allow 2 hours one way
Usually open March through December
Topographic map:
U.S.G.S. Hood River, Oreg.-Wash.
15'   1957

The perfect time to climb Dog Mountain is mid to late May when the acres of open slopes near the summit are smothered with the big yellow blooms of balsamroot — a visual feast for eye and camera. Since the blossoming time varies from year to year, many hikers hedge by first driving to the Starvation Creek Rest Area on I-84 near milepost 55 and peer through binoculars across the Columbia River to the alleged flower fields. If they have not reached their peak, an alternate trek is taken and the ritual is repeated the next week.

But Dog Mountain has more to offer than its annual flower show. Like Hamilton Mountain (No. 1) and Beacon Rock (No. 2), it is a particularly good hike in late fall and early spring since snow seldom remains below the summit area and the sun's wan rays warm its slopes while missing those on the Oregon side. Sights enjoyed during the climb and from the summit include the Columbia River, Mounts Hood, Adams and St. Helens, the lesser outcroppings of Mt. Defiance (No. 33) and Wind Mountain and the Hood River Valley. Unless you are not enervated by hot weather and don't mind the possibility of disturbing snoozing rattlesnakes, avoid Dog Mountain from the end of May through August. However, paradoxically, at other times carry extra clothing as a nippy wind frequently blows across the summit area.

Proceed on Washington 14 for 12 miles east of the Bridge of the Gods across from Cascade Locks to a large parking area off the north side of the highway where a sign identifies the Dog Mountain Trail.

Walk east along an old road for 100 yards to a sign on the left marking the route. As of 1980, the Dog Mountain Trail No. 147 also is the route of the Pacific Crest Trail No. 2000 that is in the process of being relocated to the west so backpackers following the route won't have the long highway walk to (or from) the Bridge of the Gods.

Turn left (north) and wind up a steady, moderate grade in nine switchbacks of varying lengths to a grassy bench. During the climb you can look across the Columbia River to the route of the Starvation Ridge Trail (No. 34) and above it to antenna-topped Mt. Defiance.

Follow the level path north along the bench then climb along a faint road to a second, considerably smaller clearing where a sign points to water about 50 feet to the east, the only source along the trip. Resume climbing steeply along the old road bed then level off and head east on a trail through a swath of deciduous growth. Continue traversing, now in a coniferous forest, then climb again. Switchback left, traverse to the north, switchback right and pass through a second deciduous area. Re-enter deep woods, switchback three times and wind up along a hillside of large, widely spaced evergreens.

Make one last turn and traverse the open slope of possible balsamroot blooms to a small, level viewpoint where a tidy white lookout cabin once stood. The hikes to Larch Mountain (No's. 9, 10 and 12), Tanner Butte (No. 21), Nesmith Point (No. 15), Chinidere Mountain (see No. 26), Green Point Mountain (No. 30), Mt. Defiance (No. 33) and the Wygant Trail (No. 35) also visit the sites of former lookouts. Indian Mountain, Pepper Mountain, Aldrich Butte and Greenleaf Peak in the Gorge area also once supported lookouts. These structures were removed when aerial surveillance replaced them as the more effective method of fire detection. As interesting and charming as these towers and ground houses were, Forest Service personnel knew they would become eyesores and hazards as they deteriorated, thus they have followed a policy of destroying the unused structures.

The main trail continues east into woods then heads north to Grassy Knoll and beyond. For a higher perspective of the surrounding terrain, head northwest from the viewpoint along a path that follows a low ridge crest then climbs very steeply along the open slopes.

14

Dog Mountain

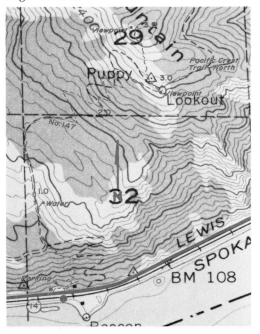

15

4   LATOURELL FALLS

One-half day trip
Distance: 2.1 miles round trip
Elevation gain: 500 feet
High Point: 700 feet
Allow 1½ hours round trip
Usually open February through December
Topographic map:
   U.S.G.S. Bridal Veil, Wash.-Oreg.
   15'   1954

Latourell Falls is the most westerly of the many spectacular cascades in the Gorge accessible from the Old Columbia River Highway. Although most of the publicly owned land south of the river is managed by the U.S. Forest Service, a few portions, such as the area around Latourell Falls, belong to the State. You can cover all the trails within the two adjacent parks (Guy W. Talbot and George W. Joseph) by making a 2.1 mile loop that climbs above the first falls to the upper one, then returns under a highway bridge and passes the huge bowl at the base of the lower cascade. By combining this circuit with other short trips in the vicinity, such as the Horsetail-Oneonta Creek Loop (No. 11) and the Elowah Falls Trail (No. 16) in Yeon State Park, you would have a full day of easy and very scenic hiking.

From the west proceed on I-84 to the Bridal Veil Exit 28 and follow the exit road 0.2 mile to its junction with the Old Columbia River Highway. Turn right and drive 2.9 miles to a sign stating *Latourell Creek Trail* and a large parking area off the south side of the road. Coming from the east, take the Ainsworth Park Interchange, Exit 35, and travel west on the Old Columbia River Highway 9.5 miles to the parking area for Latourell Falls. If you're approaching along the Old Highway from the west, the parking area is 2.4 miles east of Crown Point.

Climb on the paved trail 200 feet to a view of lower Latourell Falls, named for a prominent settler in the area, then turn left and begin traversing up the slope of a large, wooded bowl along a now un-asphalted surface. Make one set of switchbacks and continue up past a viewpoint to the junction of the parallel trails to upper Latourell Falls.

To follow the easterly half of the loop first, keep left, climb gradually and near 0.5 mile make one set of switchbacks. Cross two small foot bridges, drop slightly to a third, then walk on the level to a fourth. Cross a span at the base of the cascade and travel on the level along the western part of the loop then descend in two switchbacks and continue downhill to the junction above the bridge over Latourell Creek at 0.3 mile. If you want to end the loop here, cross the bridge and return along the route you followed up.

To reach the trailhead without retracing your steps, keep left at the junction above the west end of the bridge at 0.3 mile and climb for 150 feet to a viewpoint. Continue up in one set of short switchbacks to a second overlook then travel on a crest through a tunnel of deciduous growth. Traverse downhill along a stately forested slope, switchback once, pass an old water tank and wind down to the highway.

You can walk east along the highway for 500 feet to the parking area or, if you'd like a little more hiking, look for a trail heading down from the north side of the road west of the highway bridge. Follow the path down to the picnic area then turn right at a sign pointing to Latourell Falls parking area. Soon curve south and walk under the highway bridge whose gracefully arched supports create the effect of a massive cathedral. Continue parallel to Latourell Creek then cross a foot bridge near the pool at the base of the lower falls. A semi-circle of a 300-foot high wall of columnar basalt towers above you here. Climb the final short distance to the parking area.

Lower Latourell Falls

5
ANGELS REST
to WAHKEENA FALLS

One day trip
Distance: 6.4 miles one way
Elevation gain: 1,850 feet; loss 100 feet
High Point: 1,800 feet
Allow 4 hours one way
Usually open March through mid-December
Topographic map:
 U.S.G.S. Bridal Veil, Wash.-Oreg.
 15'   1954

Hikers who don't want to make the entire traverse find Angels Rest at 2.2 miles a popular destination. On a calm day the large flat, treeless summit area is a fine place to leisurely study the views of the western end of the Gorge and down the Columbia River toward Portland. A little picnic area at 3.0 miles and Wahkeena Spring 1.9 miles farther also are enjoyable places to end the hike. Or, if you want a longer rather than a shorter trip, refer to Trail No's. 6, 7 and 8 for possible extensions. Since this hike begins and ends at the Old Columbia River Highway, it is ideal for a car shuttle.

From the west drive on I-84 to the Bridal Veil Exit 28 (not accessible to westbound traffic) and follow the exit road 0.2 mile to its junction with the Old Columbia River Highway. Leave your car in the large parking area between the two roads. If you are establishing a car shuttle, continue east 2.5 miles to the parking area at Wahkeena Falls. From the east, take I-84 to the Ainsworth Park Interchange, Exit 35, and follow west on the Old Columbia River Highway for 7.0 miles to the parking area for the Angels Rest Trail. If you're approaching from the west along the Old Highway, the trailhead is 5.0 miles east of Crown Point.

Cross the Old Columbia River Highway to the signed trail traversing up a bank. Walk through woods then swtichback twice and traverse a rocky slope where you can see down to the Columbia River and the cliffs of Cape Horn on the Washington side. Several yards beyond the scree keep left where an old section of the route goes right and climb into a side canyon.

Travel above Coopey Falls near Coopey Creek then cross the stream on a bridge. Soon switchback and make a long traverse to the east along the deciduously wooded canyon wall. Switchback left and traverse to the edge of another side canyon where you can see Angels Rest. Continue up in switchbacks and traverses, alternating between the north and south sides of the ridge, then at 2.0 miles walk along an open, rocky area.

Travel through brushy vegetation, switchback then resume hiking on a tread of slabs to an unsigned junction at a narrow ridge top. To reach Angels Rest, keep straight (left), scramble over a few rocks and travel north along the crest for a few hundred feet to the summit area. This high point originally was called Fort Rock and a trail to it was in use as early as 1916.

To continue the hike to Wahkeena Falls, turn sharply right at the crest and walk along the narrow rib for a short distance. Enter coniferous woods, climb in two short switchbacks and traverse along a north facing slope. Descend slightly then travel on the level before crossing a stream and passing the small picnic area. Climb steeply for a short distance then hike on the level again.

Three quarters mile from the picnic spot cross a small footbridge and several yards beyond have a view of Mt. St. Helens. Begin descending and continue downhill in six switchbacks separated by moderately long traverses. Keep dropping then climb slightly to Wahkeena Creek and travel near it for a few hundred feet to Wahkeena Spring.

To complete the hike, continue about 300 feet to the junction of the Wahkeena Trail No. 420, turn left and begin descending. Keep left at the junction of the Vista Point Trail No. 419, ford a shallow stream at the base of Fairy Falls and cross Wahkeena Creek twice on small footbridges. Stay straight at the four-way junction of the spurs to Necktie Falls and Monument Viewpoint. Fifty feet beyond it turn sharply right and descend in eleven switchbacks. At the final one meet the junction of the Perdition Trail No. 421, turn left and continue downhill, passing Wahkeena Falls, to the highway.

Wahkeena Spring

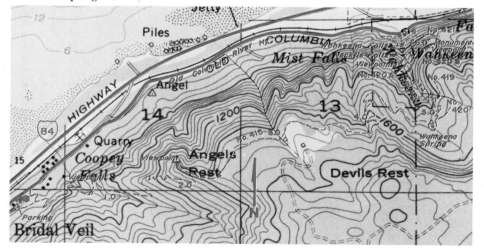

6 DEVILS REST

One day trip
Distance: 4 miles one way
Elevation gain: 2,400 feet
High Point: 2,450 feet
Allow 2 hours one way
Usually open March through November
Topographic map:
  U.S.G.S. Bridal Veil, Wash.-Oreg.
  15'   1954

Actually, the dense woods and scattered rock outcroppings at Devils Rest would be a more appropriate place of respite for elves and other fairy folk. You could nicely balance your visit here by combining it with the hike to the open, more celestial, Angels Rest (No. 5). Or, if you'd like a longer hike but don't want to backtrack or establish a car shuttle, study the maps for No's. 7 and 8 for the routes of possible loops.

Proceed on the Old Columbia River Highway 2.5 miles east from the Bridal Veil Exit 28 (not accessible to west bound traffic) off I-84 or 4.5 miles west from the Ainsworth Park Interchange, Exit 35, to the parking area at Wahkeena Falls. The trail begins just above the south side of the road at the west end of the bridge over Wahkeena Creek.

Switchback once, continue climbing past Wahkeena Falls and traverse up to the junction of the Perdition Trail No 421. Turn right and climb in ten more switchbacks to a narrow crest. Turn left and travel along the ridge top for 50 feet to the junctions of short spurs to Necktie Falls and Monument Viewpoint. Keep straight on the middle route and soon walk up the narrow canyon for a short distance, crossing Wahkeena Creek twice. Make four short switchbacks, ford a shallow stream at the base of Fairy Falls and continue winding up to the junction of the Vista Point Trail No. 419.

Since you can reach the Devils Rest Trail along either No. 419 or No. 420, a little loop is possible, and suggested. The Vista Point Trail is more varied scenically but the Wahkeena Trail passes near a good place for a food stop. If you take the Vista Point Trail, turn left, after several yards cross a stream, the last source of water along the route, and hike uphill to the crest of the ridge where an unsigned little loop goes downslope. Switchback and climb on or near the crest, traveling on the level twice, to the junction with the Wahkeena Trail. Turn left and walk 75 feet to the beginning of the trail to Devils Rest on your right.

To follow the Wahkeena Trail up from the junction above Fairy Falls, turn right, staying on Trail No. 420, and climb in four switchbacks to the junction of Trail No. 415 to Angels Rest. To reach that good food stop, turn right and take No. 415 for about 100 yards to a small clearing below the right side of the trail at Wahkeena Spring. To continue the trip to Devils Rest, turn left (east) at the junction of No's. 420 and 415 and climb steadily for 0.4 mile to the upper end of the Vista Point Trail then continue 75 feet to the beginning of the Devils Rest Trail.

Climb in seven switchbacks, continue hiking uphill then travel at an almost level grade near the rim of Wahkeena Basin. Come to the junction of the connector to the Multnomah Basin Road, keep right and continue on the level. Drop slightly to two footbridges then resume climbing and pass a view of Mounts St. Helens, Rainier and Adams, the Columbia River and Hamilton (No. 1) and Table Mountains. Keep climbing and pass an unsigned path on your right that goes about 100 yards to a small viewpoint where you can see the above landmarks plus Nesmith Point (No. 15) and the Benson Plateau (No. 26).

Stay left on the main trail and after walking about 50 yards along a faint road come to an unsigned trail climbing a bank on your right. If you intersect a second road, you've gone too far. Turn right onto the path, climb moderately and where a faint trail, the original connector to Angels Rest, joins from the west, turn right again. Go the final several yards to the whimsical sign that identifies Devils Rest.

Columbia River from Monument Viewpoint

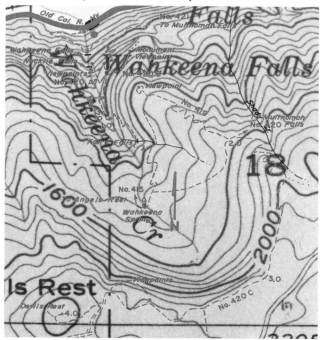

7 MULTNOMAH-PERDITION LOOP

One-half day trip
Distance: 3 miles round trip
Elevation gain: 1,000 feet
High Point: 950 feet
Allow 2 hours round trip
Usually open February through December
Topographic map:
 U.S.G.S. Bridal Veil, Wash.-Oreg.
 15'   1954

Combining the maps for the Multnomah-Perdition Loop and the Multnomah-Wahkeena Loop (No. 8) shows an intimidating maze of trails between Multnomah and Wahkeena Falls. Indeed, it is the densest network of routes in the Gorge and you could spend two delightful sessions untangling this scenic web. Actually, you can cover all the routes in one day but part of the charm of these trips is to inspect every side spur and viewpoint. These trails are among the most popular in the Gorge so, if you want more solitude, do the hikes on a weekday. The area is particularly lovely in late fall.

The Perdition Trail is the lower, and shorter by 2.0 miles, of the two east-west trails that connect the north-south routes that begin from Multnomah and Wahkeena Falls. It's a scenic and varied little trail that offers many viewpoints of the Columbia River and interesting features, such as two flights of stairs.

Drive on I-84 to the Multnomah Falls Interchange, Exit 31, and leave your car in the parking area. Walk through a tunnel under the east bound lanes and cross the Old Columbia River Highway that you also can take to reach the trailhead.

Wind up the paved trail that begins just east of the stone restaurant and gift shop and cross the graceful bridge at the top of Lower Multnomah Falls. Traverse out of the side canyon and climb in almost a dozen switchbacks along a north facing slope. The trail that heads east from the first switchback is part of the route that eventually will traverse the south side of the Columbia Gorge from Wahkeena Falls to Wyeth.

Go over a crest and descend in one switchback. Where the pavement ends a path goes sharply right to an overlook at the top of Multnomah Falls. A couple hundred feet beyond the spur the main trail crosses Multnomah Creek on a bridge and several yards farther comes to the junction of the Perdition Trail No. 421. Trail No. 441 travels upstream beside Multnomah Creek, passes the Wahkeena Trail No. 420, and continues to Larch Mountain (see No's. 9 and 10).

Turn right and travel above Multnomah Creek. Continue traversing to a spur on your right that heads downslope to a viewpoint. Descend gradually along the main trail, cross a footbridge and begin dropping more steeply. As the grade levels off keep left where a path, a section of the former tread, angles back to the right and soon stops.

Climb a short distance and pass a trail on your right that goes to a high viewpoint. Continue up the spine of a small ridge then walk along the summit before descending on wide, long steps with wooden risers. Travel through a lovely sylvan setting to a steep stairway. At its bottom turn left and traverse 0.1 mile to the junction of the Wahkeena Trail.

Keep right and continue traversing. Begin traveling on a paved surface just before coming to the bridge near the base of Wahkeena Falls. Descend in one switchback to just above the Old Columbia River Highway. To reach your starting point, cross the bridge over Wahkeena Creek and continue west along the trail for 0.5 mile, traveling in woods parallel to, but above, the road.

Wahkeena Falls

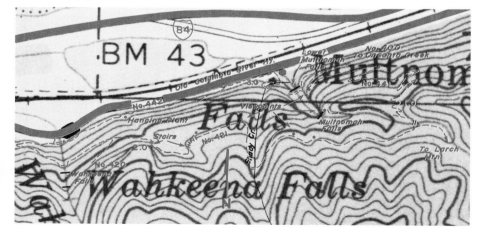

8 MULTNOMAH-WAHKEENA LOOP

One-half day trip
Distance: 5 miles round trip
Elevation gain: 1,550 feet
High Point: 1,600 feet
Allow 3 hours round trip
Usually open February through December
Topographic map:
  U.S.G.S. Bridal Veil, Wash.-Oreg.
  15'   1954

The Multnomah-Wahkeena Loop is the trip to take when you're in the mood for moseying along and investigating every viewpoint and side spur. By studying both this map and the one for the Multnomah-Perdition Loop (No. 7) you can see that you could return to your starting point along Trail No. 421 rather than No. 442.

Proceed on I-84 to the Multnomah Falls Interchange, Exit 31, and leave your car in the large parking area. Walk through a tunnel under the east bound lanes and cross the Old Columbia River Highway that you also could take to reach the trailhead.

Wind up the paved trail that begins east of the stone restaurant and gift shop and cross the bridge above the lower falls. Climb in about a dozen switchbacks along the north facing slope. The trail that heads east from the first turn is part of the route that eventually will traverse the south side of the Columbia Gorge at a low elevation from Wahkeena Falls to Wyeth. Go over a crest, descend in one switchback and keep left at the end of the pavement where a spur heads right to an overlook at the top of the falls. Cross a bridge over Multnomah Creek and come to the junction of the Perdition Trail No. 421.

Keep left and travel near Multnomah Creek. Walk under a rock overhang just before coming near the base of Upper Multnomah Falls. Wind up in several short switchbacks then traverse and come to the junction of the Wahkeena Trail No. 420. Trail No. 441 continues to Larch Mountain (see No's. 9 and 10).

Turn right and traverse uphill then curve onto the north facing slope. Continue a gradual climb, cross Shady Creek and come to the junction on your left of Trail No. 420C that rises for 2.0 miles, gaining 800 feet, to Devils Rest (No. 6). Seventy-five feet farther pass the junction of the Vista Point Trail No. 419 that rejoins the Wahkeena Trail just above Fairy Falls. If you decide to stay on the Wahkeena Trail, keep straight (left) and descend to the junction of Trail No. 415 to Angels Rest (No. 5). A good place for lunch is about 100 yards west along No. 415 at Wahkeena Spring.

To resume the loop, turn north at the junction of Trail No. 415 to Angels Rest at 3.1 miles and descend along Trail No. 420. At the fourth switchback pass the lower end of the Vista Point Trail and switchback five more times to the ford of the shallow stream at the base of Fairy Falls. Continue down in four more short switchbacks and cross Wahkeena Creek on a small bridge. Walk along the narrow canyon floor and recross the stream. Then, after several hundred feet, come to a four-way junction where a spur on the left descends 0.1 mile, loosing 200 feet of elevation, to a narrow, fenced ledge at the lip of Necktie Falls. The path on the right climbs 0.1 mile to Monument Viewpoint above Benson State Park.

To complete the hike continue north from the four way junction along the crest for 50 feet then curve sharply right and begin descending. At the eleventh switchback come to the junction of the Perdition Trail No. 421. If you aren't planning to follow this route, turn left and traverse. Cross the bridge near the base of Wahkeena Falls and continue descending to just above the Old Columbia River Highway. To reach your starting point, cross the bridge over Wahkeena Creek and continue west along the trail for 0.5 mile, traveling in woods parallel to, but above, the road.

Necktie Falls

9   MULTNOMAH CREEK TRAIL to LARCH MOUNTAIN

One day trip
Distance: 7 miles one way
Elevation gain: 4,020 feet
High Point: 4,075 feet
Allow 4 hours one way
Usually open May through November
Topographic map:
  U.S.G.S. Bridal Veil, Wash.-Oreg.
  15'   1954

All trails don't really lead to Larch Mountain, but frequently when hiking in the western end of the Columbia Gorge it seems so. In fact, you can reach Larch Mountain, sooner or later, along ten trails, specifically No's. 5 through 14, with the Multnomah Creek Trail being the most direct. From Sherrard Point at the north edge of the summit area you'll have the most far ranging panorama in the Gorge: besides Mounts Hood, St. Helens, Rainier, Adams, Jefferson and the Three Sisters, you can see a considerable way up and down the Columbia River. For a change of scene you could follow the two mile longer, exceptionally attractive Franklin Ridge Trail (No. 10) on the return or, since a road goes to Larch Mountain, you could do the trip one way only.

Drive on I-84 to the Multnomah Falls Interchange, Exit 31, and leave your car in the large parking area. Walk under the east bound lanes and cross the Old Columbia River Highway that you also could take to reach the trailhead.

Wind up the paved trail that begins east of the stone building, cross the bridge above the lower falls then climb in almost one dozen switchbacks along the north facing slope. The trail that heads east from the first turn is part of the route that eventually will traverse at a low elevation from Wahkeena Falls to Wyeth. Go over a crest, descend a short distance, keeping left at the end of the pavement where a spur goes to an overlook at the top of the falls, cross a bridge over Multnomah Creek and come to the junction of the Perdition Trail No. 421 (No. 7).

Turn left and travel near attractive Multnomah Creek. Walk under a rock overhang along a built-up section of trail just before coming near the base of Upper Multnomah Falls. Wind up in several short switchbacks then traverse to the junction of the Wahkeena Trail No. 420 (No. 8).

Keep straight (left) and after several hundred yards cross Multnomah Creek on a high bridge. Traverse above the stream at a moderate grade, level off, cross two neighboring side streams and come to the junction of the High and Low Water Trails. You can tell if the latter, that is shorter and involves no climbing, is feasible by continuing along it for several yards and peering around the rock wall. If you take the upper trail, keep right at a path to Cougar Rock. A short distance beyond where the High and Low Water Trails rejoin, keep right at another path to Cougar Rock and a few hundred feet farther come to Road N-102. Several yards along the road a small sign on the left points to a campsite.

Cross the road and resume hiking on Trail No. 441 for about 0.2 mile to the Franklin Ridge Trail No. 427 (No. 10). Keep right (straight) and 150 yards farther come to a ford that is a problem only during periods of heavy runoff. Make two small switchbacks and continue 0.3 mile to the second, and final, ford. Switchback then soon traverse a large scree slope. Re-enter woods and continue up to the junction of Multnomah Creek Way No. 444 that connects with the Franklin Ridge Trail.

Stay straight (right) and continue uphill along a sometimes rough tread. Walk on the level and pass the site of a former shelter just before coming to a spur from the Larch Mountain Road. Cross the bed and resume climbing along the mostly smooth trail. Farther on you'll glimpse the rocky face of Sherrard Point. Skirt the edge of the picnic area, pass some restrooms and come to the southwest corner of the parking area at the end of the Larch Mountain Road. Walk to its northwest corner and follow the trail that begins there for 0.3 mile to Sherrard Point and those extensive views.

Upper Multnomah Falls

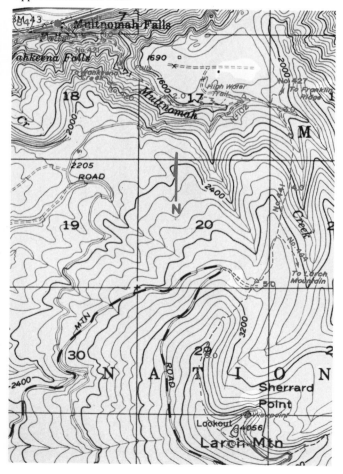

10 FRANKLIN RIDGE TRAIL to LARCH MOUNTIAN

One day trip
Distance: 9 miles one way
Elevation gain: 4,270 feet; loss 160 feet
High Point: 4,075 feet
Allow 5½ hours one way
Usually open May through November
Topographic map:
   U.S.G.S. Bridal Veil, Wash.-Oreg.
   15'   **1954**

The Franklin Ridge Trail is the most scenic of the several ways to reach Larch Mountain. By returning along the Multnomah Creek Trail (No. 9) you can enjoy different terrain and lessen the descent by two miles.

Proceed on I-84 to the Multnomah Falls Interchange, Exit 31, and leave your car in the large parking area. Walk under the east bound lanes through a tunnel and cross the Old Columbia River Highway that you also can take to reach the trailhead.

Wind up the paved trail that begins east of the stone restaurant and gift shop and cross the graceful bridge above the lower falls. Traverse out of the side canyon then climb in almost a dozen switchbacks along a north facing slope. The trail that heads east from the first turn is part of the route that eventually will traverse at a low elevation from Wahkeena Falls to Wyeth. Go over a crest, descend a short distance, keeping left at the end of the pavement where a spur goes right to an overlook at the top of the falls, cross a bridge over Multnomah Creek and come to the junction of the Perdition Trail No. 421 (No. 7). Turn left and travel near Multnomah Creek. Near the base of Upper Multnomah Falls wind up in several short switchbacks then traverse to the junction of the Wahkeena Trail No. 420 (No. 8).

Keep straight (left) and after several hun-dred yards cross Multnomah Creek on a high bridge. Traverse above the stream, level off then cross two neighboring side creeks and come to the junction of the High and Low Water Trails. If the stream flow is low enough, the latter is easier as it involves no uphill. If you take the upper trail, keep right at a path to Cougar Rock. A short distance beyond where the High and Low Water Trails rejoin, keep right at another path to Cougar Rock and a few hundred feet farther come to Road N-102. Cross the road and resume hiking on Trail No. 441 for about 0.2 mile to the junction of the Franklin Ridge Trail.

Turn left and go over a low crest then travel along the southeastern edge of Multnomah Basin. Begin climbing along a slope and at the top of the ridge come to a large clearing with fine views both east and west. Turn right at the sign in the middle of the meadow and begin climbing moderately steeply along the crest. During the next mile you'll have occasional good views of landmarks to the east. Climb through a smaller clearing then resume traveling up through woods, still following the ridge top. Eventually, leave the crest and traverse through an exceptionally attractive forest to the junction of the Oneonta Trail No. 424 (No. 12). Keep straight (right), soon drop slightly then wind through a corridor of blowdown. Climb and descend for short distances then walk gradually uphill to the second junction with No. 424, the route of a possible short loop on the return.

Turn right and go downhill for about 300 yards to an easy ford of shallow, wide East Multnomah Creek. Resume climbing and travel along a ridge crest then descend to the junction of Multnomah Creek Way No. 444 that connects with the Multnomah Creek Trail that you followed for the first 2.7 miles, another possible loop.

Stay left and soon pass near a large meadow. Begin winding up along a rooty, rocky trail then continue climbing through woods on a smoother tread. Come to an old logging railroad bed and follow it for 0.7 mile to the upper junction with the Oneonta Trail No. 424. Turn right and climb moderately for another 0.7 mile to the Larch Mountain Road, turn right again and take it for 0.3 mile to its end. The 0.3 mile long trail to Sherrard Point, that offers the most far ranging views in the Gorge, begins at the northwest corner of the parking area and the Multnomah Creek Trail No. 441 starts from the southwest edge.

Trailside vegetation

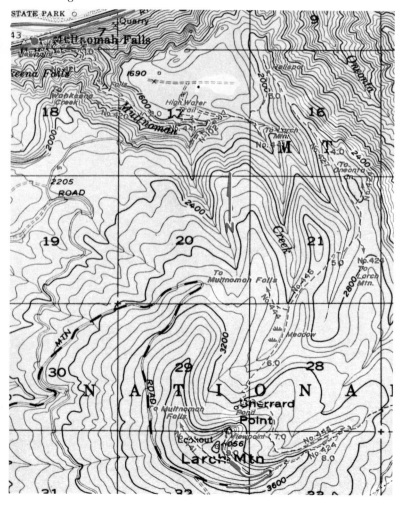

11 HORSETAIL FALLS-ONEONTA CREEK LOOP

One-half day trip
Distance: 2.7 miles round trip
Elevation gain: 500 feet
High Point: 450 feet
Allow 1½ hours round trip
Usually open February through December
Topographic map:
U.S.G.S. Bridal Veil, Wash.-Oreg.
15'   1954

This scenic and charming loop is one of the most appealing short trips in the Gorge. In addition to traveling through exceptionally attractive woods, the route goes behind a waterfall, traverses a rocky slope inhabited by shy conies, passes several overlooks and affords views of both the upper and lower portions of very narrow Oneonta Gorge.

Drive on the Old Columbia River Highway 2.5 miles east of Multnomah Falls or 1.3 miles west from the Ainsworth Park Interchange, Exit No. 35, off I-84 to turnouts on either side of the road at Horsetail Falls. A large wooden sign showing the trail network in the area marks the beginning of the hike.

Traverse up to the east and continue climbing moderately in five switchbacks. Trail No. 400, which you'll see on the third turn, heads east to the Ainsworth interchange and is a section of the low elevation traverse that eventually will extend from Wahkeena Falls to Wyeth. Walk on level along the face of a moss, fern and, in spring, wildflower covered wall then curve into the small side canyon that holds Ponytail Falls. Walk behind the falls through a low ceilinged chamber. The rock here, weaker than the layers above and below, has been more susceptible to erosion by freezing and thawing and flowing water. Traverse out of the side canyon then walk on the level along the face of the Gorge. Where the trail forks you can follow either branch. The path to the right goes to a view of the Columbia River and a backwash area of grass and cottonwoods then rejoins the main route.

Traverse high along the east side of Oneonta Gorge then wind down in six short switchbacks to the bridge across the defile. You'll have a particularly interesting view down the narrow gorge at the second turn. The origin of this canyon is the same as the cavern behind Ponytail Falls except that here the weaker rock is in a vertical instead of a horizontal configuration.

Climb in one set of switchbacks to the Oneonta Trail (No's. 12 and 14). If you want a slightly longer trip you could travel south up this route for 1.0 mile to Triple Falls. To complete the loop, turn right and climb gradually along the face of the ridge. Be watching for a path on your right where the main trail curves to the west. This spur passes three viewpoints that afford extensive views up and down the Columbia Gorge then loops back to the main route. If you stay on the Oneonta Trail you may hear and see conies along the section of rocky terrain just before crossing over a ridge crest where the side path rejoins the trail. Descend and switchback right at the junction of the section of Trail No. 400 that connects the Oneonta Creek and Multnomah Creek (see No's. 7 through 10) Trails.

Continue traversing down, keeping right where an unsigned trail goes left to the highway, and head east until you reach the pavement. If you haven't established a car shuttle, walk east along the shoulder, passing the lower end of Oneonta Gorge, for 0.5 mile to your starting point. Late in the summer when Oneonta Creek is its lowest many pick their way along the canyon floor to the base of the falls.

Trail west of Oneonta Creek

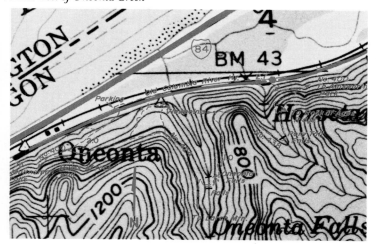

12 ONEONTA CREEK TRAIL to LARCH MOUNTAIN

One day trip
Distance: 8 miles one way
Elevation gain: 4,225 feet; loss 200 feet
High Point: 4,075 feet
Allow 5 hours one way
Usually open May through November
Topographic map:
    U.S.G.S. Bridal Veil, Wash.-Oreg.
    15'   1954

The Oneonta Creek Trail probably is the most demanding of the three direct routes to Larch Mountain as the grade is very steep between 2.5 and 3.8 miles and the route requires two fords of Oneonta Creek. However, from mid-summer through late fall you should be able to negotiate these crossings without getting your feet wet. To add variety to an already scenic trip, a little loop is possible between the 4.1 and 6.9 mile points along a section of the Franklin Ridge Trail (No. 10). If you establish a short car shuttle, you can return along the Multnomah Creek (No. 9) or Franklin Ridge Trails or, since a road also goes to the summit of Larch Mountain, you could do the trip one way only.

Proceed on the Old Columbia River Highway 2.0 miles east of Multnomah Falls or 1.8 miles west from the Ainsworth Park Interchange, Exit 35, off I-84 to a wide shoulder for parking across the road from a sign stating *Oneonta Trail.*

Hike uphill to the west, keeping left where a path descends back to the highway, then switchback left. The trail to the right here is a section of No. 400, the west-east, low elevation traverse that eventually will go from Wahkeena Falls to Wyeth. Continue climbing to a crest where a side trail heads left past three viewpoints and then loops back to the main route. Traverse a rocky slope, curve into Oneonta Creek canyon and come to the junction of the Horsetail Falls Trail No. 438 (No.

11).

Keep right and climb at a steady grade along the forested canyon wall. Make one set of switchbacks and continue traveling uphill then begin descending just before a view of Triple Falls. Wind down in two short switchbacks then a few hundred feet farther come to the first ford. Be cautious as some of the rocks may be slippery.

Follow up along the east side of the stream then make two sets of switchbacks, separated by a traverse, and come to the second ford where you can walk (or scoot) across a log. Rise in two short switchbacks to the junction of the Horsetail Creek Trail No. 425 (No. 14).

Keep right and climb through an open, rocky area then begin a long traverse to the west. Rise very steeply in three switchbacks, curve onto an east facing slope and climb at a more reasonable grade, crossing a few rocky swaths. At the end of one large scree slope switchback, traverse, then switchback again, and pass some viewpoints over the upper portions of Oneonta Canyon. Climb steeply in four switchbacks, wind up to a broad crest then descend briefly to the junction with the Franklin Ridge Trail No. 427.

Turn left, drop briefly and wind through a corridor of blowdown from the infamous Columbus Day Storm of 1962. Climb and descend for short distances before walking gradually uphill to the junction of Trail No. 446 that connects with No. 444, the route of the possible short loop.

Stay left (straight), climb over a small crest then descend and travel at a gradual grade before dropping again to a stream crossing. Climb then go downhill to a second ford. Rise considerably more steeply, make five short switchbacks and about 200 feet beyond the last one come to the junction of Bell Creek Way that may be unsigned. Turn right and traverse to the ford of a small stream, descend briefly then walk on the level to a road.

Turn right and stay on the road for 200 yards to a sign on your left marking the resumption of the Oneonta Trail. Turn left and soon begin climbing along a ridge crest. Come to an old logging railroad grade and the junction of the upper end of No. 444. Keep straight (left) and continue uphill for 0.7 mile to the Larch Mountain Road. Turn right and walk 0.3 mile up to the road's end. For one of the most far ranging views in the Gorge, follow the 0.3 mile long trail that begins from the northwest corner of the parking area to Sherrard Point.

Oneonta Creek

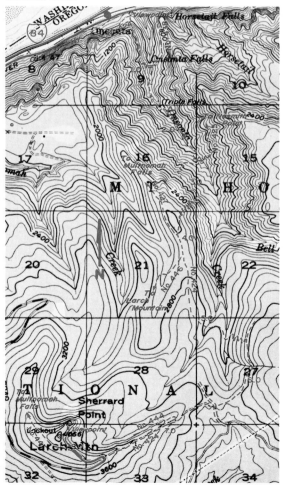

13 ROCK of AGES RIDGE

One day trip
Distance: 3 miles one way
Elevation gain: 2,980 feet
High Point: 3,020 feet
Allow 2½ to 3 hours one way
Usually open late May through November
Topographic map:
U.S.G.S. Bridal Veil, Wash.-Oreg.
15'   1954

For steep, unremitting uphill the Rock of Ages Ridge Trail is a first cousin to the Munra Point (No. 17) and Ruckel Ridge (No. 24) climbs. After 0.3 mile of moderate uphill, you rise 2,175 feet in 1.6 miles. To see more scenery and save your knees from the rigors of the descent you can return along one of two possible routes: The first follows the Horsetail Creek Trail (No. 14) back to your starting point and would add 5.0 miles. Since this loop crosses Oneonta Creek three times, the circuit is best done when the stream flow is low. The second, along the Nesmith Point Trail (No. 15), is 4.5 miles longer and would necessitate a short car shuttle. Carry water.

Drive on the Old Columbia River Highway 2.5 miles east of Multnomah Falls or 1.3 miles west from the Ainsworth Park Interchange, Exit 35, off I-84 to turnouts on both sides of the road at Horsetail Falls. A large wooden sign showing the trail network in the area marks the beginning of the trail.

Traverse up to the east and continue climbing moderately in five switchbacks. Trail No. 400 that continues east at the third turn goes to the Ainsworth interchange and is a section of the low elevation traverse that eventually will connect Wahkeena Falls and Wyeth. Walk on the level along the face of a moss, fern and, in spring, wildflower-covered wall then just as you curve into the side canyon holding Ponytail Falls, look up to your left for an unsigned use path climbing along the wooded crest.

Scramble onto this trail and quickly gain elevation. Where you come to a cluster of junctions continue uphill then at a fork where a path heads east toward a ridge on the skyline, bear right and keep climbing. Come to a small, open perch. A path on the left traverses north for a few hundred feet then winds steeply up for several yards to a natural arch of conglomerate on the rim of a sheer wall.

The main route traverses an open slope and reenters woods before resuming the steep climb. Continue along the crest then scramble up a vertical slope a few yards high to the edge of the Devils Backbone. A path traverses the east side of the outcropping for those who don't feel comfortable walking along the exposed spine. A flat, grassy area at the south end of the formation with views of Mt. Adams, Hamilton (No. 1) and Table Mountains, Beacon Rock (No. 2), Bonneville Dam and St. Peters Dome is a good spot for a snack stop.

Reenter woods and climb along the crest at a considerably more moderate grade. The angle steepens then becomes gradual again where you can see Rock of Ages across the chasm to the east. The exposed face of this outcropping shows the many successive layers of lava that have formed the rock in this section of the Gorge.

Drop slightly then resume a steep ascent. Eventually, the crest broadens and the character of the woods changes. At 1.9 miles the trail comes to the edge of the basin west of Yeon Mountain. Walk near the rim at a gradual grade for one mile to the junction of the Horsetail Creek Trail. Turn right to make the loop back to your starting spot or turn left to reach the Nesmith Point Trail.

The Arch

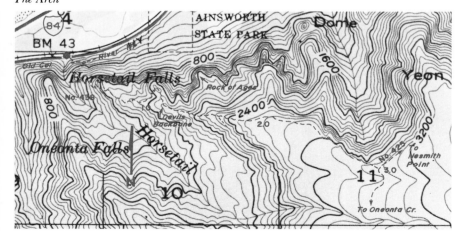

14 HORSETAIL CREEK TRAIL

One day trip or backpack
Distance: 9 miles one way
Elevation gain: 4,200 feet; loss 350 feet
High Point: 3,880 feet
Allow 5½ to 6 hours one way
Usually open June through November
Topographic map:
  U.S.G.S. Bridal Veil, Wash.-Oreg.
  15'   1954

The east-west oriented Horsetail Creek Trail between Oneonta Creek and Nesmith Point (No. 15) can be hiked one way by establishing a short car shuttle or you can make a loop along all but the most easterly two miles of the Horsetail Creek Trail by following the Rock of Ages Ridge Trail (No. 13) up and returning along the Horsetail route. For both variations it is recommended you do the Rock of Ages Ridge or Nesmith Point ways first. There are three fords of Oneonta Creek between 1.9 and 2.9 miles but if the water level is low and if a log is across the highest ford you should manage these crossings without getting your feet wet.

Proceed on the Old Columbia River Highway 2.5 miles east of Multnomah Falls or 1.3 miles west from the Ainsworth Park Interchange, Exit 35, off I-84 to turnouts on either side of the road at Horsetail Falls. A large wooden sign with a map off the south shoulder just east of the falls identifies the trail.

Head up to the east and continue climbing moderately in five switchbacks. Trail No. 400, which continues east at the third turn, goes to the Ainsworth interchange and is a section of the low elevation traverse that eventually will connect Wahkeena Falls and Wyeth. Walk on the level along the face of a moss and fern covered wall then curve into the small side canyon that holds Ponytail Falls. Walk behind the falls, traverse out of the side canyon then travel on the level, following either branch where the trail forks. Traverse high along the east side of Oneonta Gorge then wind down in six short switchbacks to the bridge across the defile. Climb in one set of switchbacks to the Oneonta Creek Trail No. 424 (No. 12) and turn left.

Generally travel uphill, making one set of switchbacks, then begin a slight descent just before the first view of Triple Falls. Wind down and a few hundred feet farther come to the first ford. Be cautious as some of the rocks may be slippery. Make two sets of switchbacks, separated by a traverse, cross a few small side streams and come to the second ford where you can walk (or scoot) across a log. Climb in two short switchbacks to the junction of the Horsetail Creek Trail. The Oneonta Creek Trail continues up to Larch Mountain.

Keep left and descend to the final ford. Wind up and begin a traverse along which you'll cross five small side streams. Climb moderately in nine switchbacks then, after a long traverse, pass a viewpoint on a nubbin to your right and make six more switchbacks. At the last turn you can see the hulk of Larch Mountain (see No's. 9, 10 and 12) to the west.

Continue uphill then begin traveling at a more gradual grade across an area of gentle contours. At 5.7 miles come to Horsetail Creek. Traverse out of the side canyon holding the stream and climb slightly to the ford of the Middle Fork of Horsetail Creek. Continue uphill then descend briefly to the final crossing, the East Fork of Horsetail Creek. Wind through a more open area of deciduous growth then rise moderately to the unsigned junction of the Rock of Ages Ridge Trail on your left.

Keep straight (right) and walk for 0.3 mile near the rim of the Gorge. Go over the shoulder of Yeon Mountain and continue gradually uphill to an overlook at 7.9 miles directly across from Hamilton Mountain (No. 1) and Beacon Rock (No. 2). Veer away from the rim and drop slightly to Road N-122. Turn left and walk up the bed, passing a sign identifying the Nesmith Point Trail after 0.2 mile. Continue climbing along the road then near the crest curve right and follow a path for several yards to the rocky site of the former lookout.

36

Hikers near Yeon Mountain

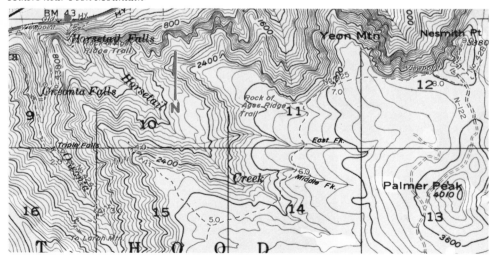

15 NESMITH POINT

One day trip
Distance: 5 miles one way
Elevation gain: 3,810 feet
High Point: 3,880 feet
Allow 3½ to 4 hours one way
Usually open June through November
Topographic maps:
　U.S.G.S. Bonneville Dam, Oreg.-Wash.
　15' 　　　　　　　　　　　　**1957**
　U.S.G.S. Bridal Veil, Wash.-Oreg.
　15' 　　　　　　　　　　　　**1954**

Nesmith Point is one of the highest places on the rim of the Columbia Gorge and from the summit area you can look down onto Beacon Rock (No. 2) and beyond to Hamilton (No. 1) and Table Mountains in Washington. You can make a loop that would add 3.5 miles of downhill hiking, involve one ford and two crossings of Oneonta Creek and necessitate a short car shuttle by returning along the Horsetail Creek Trail (No. 14). Carry water on the climb to Nesmith Point as sources along the trail are not dependable.

From the west, drive on I-84 to the Ainsworth Park Interchange, Exit 35. Turn left at the end of the exit, following the signs to Dodson and Warrendale, then after 150 feet keep right — don't go back onto the freeway. Travel east on the frontage road for 2.3 miles to a large parking area just before the road joins the eastbound lanes of the freeway. If you're approaching from the east, continue

2.7 miles west of the Bonneville Dam Interchange, Exit 40, to the Dodson-Warrendale Exit No. 37. Take it, after going under the freeway turn left and proceed 0.4 mile to the parking area.

Climb for several yards along the trail that begins at the southwestern end of the turnout, switchback left near an old water tank and 75 feet farther come to the junction of the Nesmith Trail. The route that continues straight goes to Upper and Lower Elowah Falls (No. 16). Turn right and after a short distance curve left onto an old road and follow it for several yards. Resume traveling on a trail, switchback and head in a westerly direction. Traverse a small scree slope then switchback left just before a stream that may not flow above ground all year. The trail that crosses the bridge here is a section of No. 400, the low elevation traverses from Wahkeena Falls to Wyeth. Climb in a set of short switchbacks and at 1.1 miles come to a ridge crest where a path leads left to a viewpoint.

Curve right and traverse at a more noticeable grade along the western wall of a small basin. Cross to the eastern side then return to the western slope and switchback up a narrow draw. Head west along the face of a vertical slope then climb in a second series of short switchbacks. Traverse for a short distance to the crest of a ridge, curve right and hike along the open wall of the huge upper basin. Cross to the eastern side in a long traverse then climb in several switchbacks to the rim of the basin at 3.0 miles where you can look down into McCord Creek canyon.

Curve right and traverse up the wooded slope for 0.4 mile then veer right and continue traversing, but at a more gradual grade, along the southeast facing slope. Descend slightly then resume climbing. Pass through two small, open areas then come to a sign at 4.6 miles where the trail curves sharply right. If you are making the loop and want to save 300 feet of climbing and 0.4 mile, you can bypass Nesmith Point by keeping straight (left) here and following the faint trail for 0.1 mile to Road N-122. Turn right, walk up the road for 200 yards to the sign marking Horsetail Creek Way No. 425 and turn left.

To reach Nesmith Point, turn right at the junction at 4.6 miles and climb along the main trail for a short distance to Road N-122. Turn right and wind up the road for 0.2 mile. Where you come near the rim curve right and follow a path for several yards to the rocky, tree-rimmed site of a former lookout cabin.

The Nesmith cirque from the air

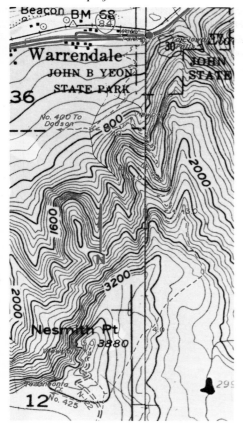

16 ELOWAH FALLS TRAIL

One-half day trip
Distance: 1 mile to Upper Elowah Falls;
0.8 mile to Lower Elowah Falls
Elevation gain: 340 feet to Upper Elowah Falls
180 feet to Lower Elowah Falls;
loss 100 feet
High Point: 500 feet
Allow ½ hour to Upper Elowah Falls
Usually open February through December
Topographic Map:
U.S.G.S. Bonneville Dam, Oreg.-Wash.
15'   1957

The short trip to Upper and Lower Elowah Falls is a delightful hike: The higher route traverses a high vertical rock face past the upper falls to a level spot beside McCord Creek and the other follows along the floor of a deep, narrow canyon to the base of the lower cascade.

From the west, proceed on I-84 to the Ainsworth Park Interchange, Exit 35. Turn left at the end of the exit, following the signs to Dodson and Warrendale, then, after 150 feet keep right — don't go back onto the freeway. Travel east on the frontage road for 2.3 miles to a large parking area just before the road joins the eastbound lanes of the freeway. If you're approaching from the east, take the Dodson-Warrendale exit 2.7 miles west of the Bonneville Dam Interchange, Exit 40, to Exit No. 37. After going under the freeway turn left and drive 0.4 mile to the parking area. The trail begins at the southwestern end of the turnout.

After several yards, switchback left near an old water tank and 75 feet farther keep left at the junction of the Nesmith Point Trail (No. 15). Walk through a corridor of deciduous growth then climb in an elegant woods of widely spaced conifers to the unsigned junction of the upper and lower trails.

To follow the higher route, turn right and travel along a mostly open slope then switchback and traverse through woods to the edge of the side canyon holding McCord Creek. Switchback and just before the next turn cross a large, old, rusted water diversion pipe. Make two more short switchbacks and come to the canyon wall. Since the trail has been blasted out of the sheer rock and metal guard rails offer protection on the exposed side, you feel quite snug while making the level traverse along the face. From this aerie you can see Mt. Adams and Table Mountain in Washington and the section of the Columbia River near Hamilton Island, the new site of the town of North Bonneville.

Travel beyond the cliff and reenter woods. Pass the upper falls, that usually plunges from the precipice as multiple streamers in contrast to the lower falls that catapults over the edge in a single, long cascade. The trail continues on the level for a short distance then stops where it comes to the bank of McCord Creek.

To reach the base of the lower falls, traverse east at a gradual downhill grade from the junction at 0.3 miles. Cross a rocky slope where you may hear the bleat of and, if you're lucky, see some conies (also called rock rabbits and pikas). These adorable little rodents inhabit a few similar rocky areas throughout the Gorge but they are timid and, unlike many chipmunks and ground squirrels, have no intention of ingratiating themselves with humans.

Curve into McCord Creek canyon and descend in six short switchbacks then walk to the head of the defile at the base of the 289 foot falls. The original route to the falls began from the Old Columbia River Highway just east of McCord Creek. Construction of the freeway destroyed this section of the road. However, much of the tread has been reopened as part of Trail No. 400, the low elevation traverses that eventually will extend from Wahkeena Falls to Wyeth. To date, the traverse extends as far east as the Columbia Gorge Work Center. McCord Creek has had several names, including Pierce and Kelly Creeks but ultimately it was named for a pioneer settler who built the first fish wheels near its mouth.

40

Elowah Falls Trail

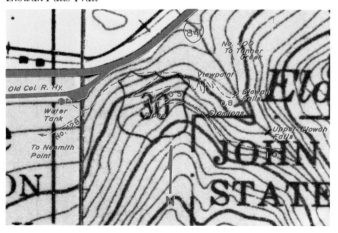

41

17 MUNRA POINT

One-half day trip
Distance: 1.3 miles one way
Elevation gain: 1,760 feet
High Point: 1,860 feet
Allow 1½ hours one way
Usually open March through December
Topographic map:
   U.S.G.S. Bonneville Dam, Oreg.-Wash.
   15'   **1957**

The short, but difficult climb to Munra Point is best done on a warm, sunny and calm day after a dry spell. Firstly, during these conditions the grassy summit ridge is a fine place for savoring a leisurely lunch and enjoying the view of the Columbia River, Mt. Adams, Beacon Rock (No. 2), Hamilton (No. 1) and Table Mountains, Bonneville Dam and the Bridge of the Gods. If you want a longer hike, you can head south along the open crest for 0.2 mile then follow an abandoned trail through woods for 1.0 mile more along the ridge top before the old route becomes faint.

Secondly, and more pragmatically, sections of the sometimes very steep route can be ex-

ceedingly slippery when wet. Even in good conditions the tread is unnerving in a few places although trees and other handholds are available for the less sure of foot. You may want to include a hiking cane or ice ax for use during the descent. Carry water as none is available along the hike.

Drive west on I-84 from the Bonneville Dam Interchange, Exit 40, about 1.0 mile to the entrance to an unofficial frontage road on your right (north). Park here, making sure you don't block the road.

Walk west to the east end of the freeway bridge over Moffett Creek, turn south and go under the high span for the eastbound lanes. Curve slightly left and look for a path that begins from a dirt bank on your right.

Climb for a couple of yards to Trail No. 400, a section of the low elevation traverse from Wahkeena Falls to Wyeth. Turn left and after about 200 feet look for a path heading up on your right.

Turn right and wind up through woods on a smooth surface then begin climbing on a rocky tread. Traverse to the southeast beneath a steep wall then at a junction turn left and begin climbing very steeply. After a couple hundred feet veer slightly right to avoid an exposed short-cut and continue up to the junction of a path to a viewpoint. Note this junction so you follow the "easier" way on the return.

Climb mostly along the crest, occasionally scrambling over rock outcroppings. The only one that would be difficult to negotiate coming down can easily be circumvented along its south side. At 1.0 mile curve left and traverse the base of a steep, low wall. Switchback right, walk to the top of the face then traverse at a gradual grade along a mostly grassy slope. About 50 feet beyond where you detour below an evergreen limb come to a junction. Take the higher trail and traverse up to the crest. (Note the alignment of the trail at the detour so you follow the correct route on your return.)

If you want to peer down onto Bonneville Dam turn left and climb a rocky rib or, to reach a good lunch spot, head south (right) along the ridge top for several hundred yards. During early spring, perky wildflowers, including a particularly good crop of wild onion, thrive on the grassy slopes. You'll be able to see just the tip of Mt. Rainier. The ridge was named for "Grandma Munra" who operated a railroad restaurant at Bonneville Dam for many years.

42

Munra Point from the air

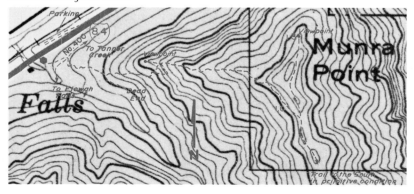

18 TANNER CREEK TRAIL

One-half day trip
Distance: 0.8 mile one way
Elevation gain: 340 feet; loss 100 feet
High Point: 380 feet
Allow ½ hour one way
Usually open February through December
Topographic map:
 U.S.G.S. Bonneville Dam, Oreg.-Wash.
 15'   1957

In 1973, attendants at the Bonneville Dam Fish Hatchery were surprised, puzzled and alarmed when the water supplied to the facility by Tanner Creek abruptly stopped. When the flow did not resume after a short time, the men became worried as hatcheries require a constant supply of fresh water, so they hiked up Tanner Creek to learn what had happened. The canyon was filled with an eerie calm and almost unearthly ambience. A short distance before Tanner Falls they found the answer: Several hundred cubic yards of the west wall had fallen away and blocked the stream, forming a small lake behind the dam. Fortunately, water began flowing through the debris before any damage was done in the hatchery. The lake, although not as large as it was soon after the avalanche, and the slide area still can be seen from the trail — an intimidating view.

The short distance and slight elevation gain of the trail to Tanner Falls belie the difficulties encountered along a few sections of the traverse. Particularly during or after rainy weather, the crossings of the several slide areas can be tricky. Consequently, the trip is most satisfactorily done during a dry spell. However, the serene glade of cedar at the base of the two part falls is ample reward for the precarious stretches. You'll probably want to spend some extra time enjoying this sylvan setting.

Proceed on I-84 to the Bonneville Dam Interchange, Exit 40. If you're coming from the west, turn right at the end of the exit and then after several yards keep right where a road climbs to the left (east). From the east, turn left at the end of the exit, go under the freeway, continue south to a junction and keep right. Stay left where a deteriorated portion of the old highway heads west. If the main route is not blocked you can drive 0.2 mile to its end at the diversion dam for the fish hatchery. Otherwise, park in the large turnout north of the gate and walk to the trailhead.

Follow the path that heads south from the installation and walk along the edge of Tanner Creek for several yards. During times of low flow you should be able to scramble from rock to rock but you might have to do some quick foot work during high water if you want to keep your feet dry. You could be so preoccupied, you might not notice the waterfall on the slope above. (It doesn't get you wet.) Begin traversing at an erratic grade but, overall, gain more elevation than you lose.

At about 0.5 mile rise and drop steeply then travel on the level for a short distance to a fork and climb to the left. At a second fork stay left again then after the path levels off veer right at the next branch and descend to the main trail. More slippage probably will occur along the preceding slide area, so follow newer routes if they seem appropriate. Traverse above the lake then wind down to the grove near the pool at the base of Tanner Falls, once named Wahclella Falls. J.T. Tanner had a donation land claim near the mouth of the creek now identified by his name.

Tanner Creek Falls

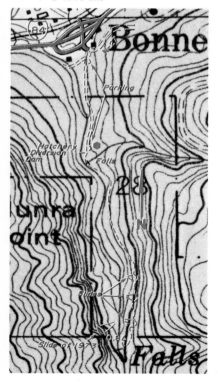

19 WAUNA POINT

One day trip
Distance: 3 miles one way
Elevation gain: 1,550 feet; loss 650 feet
High Point: 2,650 feet
Allow 2½ hours one way
Usually open April through November
Topographic map:
    U.S.G.S. Bonneville Dam, Oreg.-Wash.
    15'   1957

The actual Wauna Point is in deep woods but an exposed path winds down from this forested knob to an open, aerie perch 2,000 feet above Bonneville Dam. The narrow rock rib is just large enough for several hikers to eat their lunches while watching the traffic through the locks and identifying various landmarks including Ruckel Ridge (No. 24) and Munra Point (No. 17) directly to the east and west, the Bridge of the Gods and Table and Hamilton (No. 1) Mountains, Beacon Rock (No. 2) and Mounts Adams and Rainier in Washington.

Drive on I-84 to the Bonneville Dam Interchange, Exit 40. If you're approaching from the west, turn right at the end of the exit or, coming from the east, turn left and go under the freeway. Head south 100 feet then turn left onto a gravel road. Climb for 0.6 mile then curve right, pass a water tank and continue along Road N-27 for 1.1 miles to the head of a side canyon where a sign stating *Tanner Butte Trail* identifies the beginning of the hike. Parking spaces for a few cars are available along the shoulders.

Walk along a rocky trail for a few yards then wind up steeply in several short switchbacks. Cross a small stream, curve into a larger side canyon and cross a second creek. Traverse out of the canyon and travel along the face of an open slope where you'll be able to see Mt. Talapus in the Bull Run Reserve, Munra Point and Hamilton and Table Mountains.

Cross the power line access road and resume hiking up along a trail. Switchback left, traverse to a crest and cross from its north to south side several times then make five short switchbacks up the face of the slope. A path from the last turn goes several yards to a view of Munra, Wauneka and Nesmith Ridges. Climb at a steady grade along the west wall of a large, wooded basin. Near 2.2 miles pass a small side stream that may not flow all year and 0.1 mile farther come to the junction of the route to Wauna Point. Trail No. 401 continues to Dublin Lake and Tanner Butte (No. 21).

Turn left and walk gradually downhill through woods for 0.2 mile to a sign stating *Wauna Point 300 feet*. Of course, you can follow this route if you want, but you won't see much. Instead, turn left near the sign and descend to the northwest for several yards along a faint, blazed path. Curve sharply right several yards east of a spring, traverse below Wauna Point on a more obvious tread then wind down the steep slope in a series of very short switchbacks. Walk along the narrow ridge crest to a large outcropping, keep left and traverse up along its west side. Pick your way down a steep rock rib that is very exposed on one side to the open and flat viewpoint.

Bonneville Dam from Wauna Point

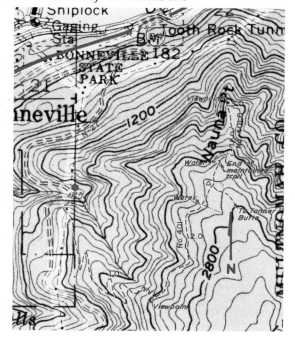

20 WAUNA VIEWPOINT

One-half day trip
Distance: 1.8 miles one way
Elevation gain: 800 feet
High Point: 940 feet
Allow 1 hour one way
Usually open February through December
Topographic map:
U.S.G.S. Bonneville Dam, Oreg.-Wash.
15'   1957

Approaching from the west proceed on I-84 to the Eagle Creek Park Exit 41. Turn right at the end of the exit then keep right where the road forks and continue several yards to a parking area on your left below picnic grounds. After the hike you'll need to drive east on the freeway for 1.4 miles to the Cascade Locks exit. If you're approaching from the east, take the Bonneville Dam Interchange, Exit 40, then go east 1.2 miles to the Eagle Creek Park Exit.

Walk east from the turnout along the road for several yards to a large suspension bridge over Eagle Creek. Cross the span and turn right or left and follow either end of the signed Nature Trail Loop. On the return, you can take the section you didn't follow earlier.

After passing the upper end of the loop (if you turned right beyond the suspension bridge) or rejoining the main trail (if you turned left), climb a short distance along the main trail, switchback and begin traversing above the fish hatchery. Curve around the face of the slope to a view of Bonneville Dam. Switchback left at the overlook and after a short distance switchback again. Continue climbing along the wooded slope then make one more set of switchbacks and resume traversing to the junction of Trail No. 402B that meets the Tanner Creek Road after 0.5 mile (see Trail No.'s 19 and 21).

Turn left, traverse then switchback five times. Cross a cleared area beneath the power lines, switchback for a final time and recross the open slope to the flat spot under the tower. Although not visible from the Viewpoint, Wauna Point is 1,200 feet directly above and is reached by taking Trail No. 19. Wauna may have been the name given by the Klickitat Indians to the mythological being who represented the Columbia River. The cement structure on the viewpoint was erected as a survey marker to aid in the construction of the new powerhouse at Bonneville Dam.

From the small level spot at the base of the power line tower on Wauna Viewpoint you'll be able to study the configurations of narrow Ruckel Ridge (No. 24) across Eagle Creek Canyon to the east, look north to Mt. Adams. And, if you're especially intrigued by man's handiwork, you can examine the workings of Bonneville Dam and locks directly below.

Ruckel Ridge from Wauna Viewpoint

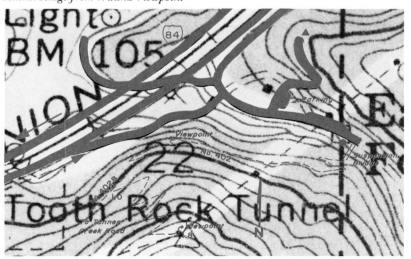

21 TANNER BUTTE

One day trip
Distance: 7.5 miles one way
Elevation gain: 3,550 feet; loss 150 feet
High Point: 4,500 feet
Allow 5 to 6 hours one way
Usually open mid-June through November
Topographic map:
  U.S.G.S. Bonneville Dam, Oreg.-Wash.
  15'   1957

Massive Tanner Butte with its treeless, rocky east side is a distinctive landmark in the Gorge from as far south as the Mt. Hood area. If the long, hard climb to the summit is not enough exercise, you could make side trips to Wauna Point (No. 19) or Dublin Lake. Also, a loop is possible on your return by following Trail No. 448 to Road N-27 and taking it back to your car. This loop, including the road walk, would add no extra mileage.

Drive on I-84 to the Bonneville Dam Interchange, Exit 40. If you're approaching from the west, turn right at the end of the exit or, coming from the east, turn left and go under the freeway. Head south 100 feet then turn left onto a gravel road. Climb for 0.6 mile then curve right, pass a water tank and continue along Road N-27 for 1.1 miles to the head of a side canyon where a sign stating *Tanner Butte Trail* identifies the beginning of the hike. Do not drive beyond this point as the road becomes very steep and is closed by a gate.

Walk along a rocky trail for a few yards then wind up steeply in several short switchbacks. Cross a small stream, curve into a larger side canyon and cross a second creek, the last dependable source of water. Traverse out of the canyon and travel along the face of an open slope where you'll be able to see pyramid-shaped Mt. Talapus in the Bull Run Reserve, Munra Point (No. 17) and Hamilton (No. 1) and Table Mountains in Washington.

Cross the power line access road and resume hiking up along a trail. Switchback left, traverse to a crest and cross from its north to south side several times, then make five short switchbacks up the face of the slope. A path from the last turn goes several yards to a view of Munra, Wauneka and Nesmith Ridges. Climb along the west wall of a large, wooded basin then near 2.2 miles pass a small side stream that may not flow all year, and 0.1 mile farther come to the junction of the spur to Wauna Point.

Keep right and continue climbing along the wide, wooded ridgecrest for 2.3 miles to the possibly unsigned junction of the Billy Goat Trail No. 448 to Road N-27, the route of the possible loop. Stay left and 120 yards farther pass a path on your left, that also may be unsigned, to Dublin Lake. To make this side trip, turn left and walk on the level for 100 feet. Descend moderately for another 100 feet and then drop steeply for several hundred yards to the wooded northwest end of the lake.

To continue the climb to Tanner Butte, follow the main trail for 0.1 mile to an old road. Turn left and walk up the bed through less dense timber along the west side of the ridge for 1.5 miles. Then drop slightly to a saddle where you can see the northwestern ridge leading to the summit of Tanner Butte.

Continue to the south end of the saddle then turn left and begin climbing cross-country near the northern edge of the slope. Although the final 0.4 mile and 500 feet of elevation gain are over trailless terrain, the going is not difficult and the correct route is obvious. Only a few remains indicate where a lookout once stood on the summit. You'll be able to identify many landmarks in the Gorge between Larch and Chinidere Mountains in addition to having views of Mt. Hood and, to the north in Washington, Mounts St. Helens, Adams and Rainier.

Hiker on Tanner Ridge

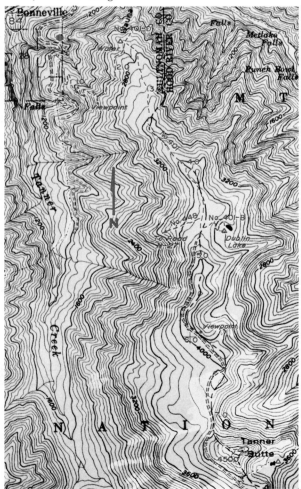

22 EAGLE CREEK-HERMAN CREEK TRAVERSE

One day trip
Distance: 8 miles one way
Elevation gain: 1,580 feet; loss 1,540 feet
High Point: 1,200 feet
Allow 4 to 4½ hours one way
Usually open February through December
Topographic map:
U.S.G.S. Bonneville Dam, Oreg.-Wash.
15'   1957

The Eagle Creek-Herman Creek Traverse, a long section of the low elevation trail between Wahkeena Falls and Wyeth, has a split personality: The first part travels furtively close to I-84 and along this stretch you occasionally have the feeling you're enjoying a city hike through exceptionally attractive, sometimes even exotic woods. But, the last five miles are far from the freeway and you seem to be in the wilds. The traverse is perfect for a car shuttle or you could end the trip at Cascade Locks if you wanted a shorter (2.8 mile) hike.

From the west proceed on I-84 to the Eagle Creek Park Exit 41, turn right at the end of the exit, drive 100 feet to a parking area where the road forks and leave your car here. To return westbound after the hike, drive 1.4 miles east to the Cascade Locks exit. Approaching from the east, take I-84 to the Bonneville Dam Interchange, Exit 40, then head east 1.2 miles to the Eagle Creek Park exit. To establish a car shuttle, refer to Trail No. 26.

Walk northeast up the paved road to the campground for 75 yards to a sign on the left shoulder identifying the Gorge Trail No. 400 to Cascade Locks. Wind up to the edge of a bluff above the freeway, turn right and follow along the fence to the north end of the campground and the junction of the trail to Buck Point and Ruckel Ridge (No. 24).

Keep left, descend to a large clearing, cross it to a section of the Old Columbia River Highway then walk along the bed to a bridge over Ruckel Creek and the beginning of the Ruckel Creek Trail (No. 23). Continue along the moss and leaf covered highway for another 0.8 mile to the beginning of Trail No. 400. Follow the trail to an open slope where you can see the Bridge of the Gods then wind through an area of slim trees and vegetation draped rock outcroppings.

Cross a narrow dirt road and continue in woods to a grassy clearing. Climb for several yards, switchback right and come to a wide dirt road. Turn left, walk along the bed to the junction of another road. Turn left again and go downhill to a cluster of signs on the right shoulder marking the resumption of the trail. If you want to go into Cascade Locks, continue down the road. Turn left at the freeway overpass, following a sign pointing to Bridge of the Gods, or stay on the road to reach the center of town.

To complete the traverse, walk east through slash above homes then head south. After 0.5 mile curve sharply left and again climb in a generally easterly direction. At 3.6 miles come to a dirt road, turn right and walk along it for about 200 feet, going under some power lines, to the continuation of the trail.

Climb gradually through woods then go over a low crest and descend at a gradual grade to a road. The unsigned Rudolph Spur Trail heading right 75 feet before the road climbs for 3.0 miles to the Ruckel Creek Trail (No. 23). A spectacular falls is a short distance to the right along the old bed. Cross the road and after several yards come to a bridge over Dry Creek. Travel uphill to an open, rocky slope, reenter woods and continue moderately uphill. Walk into a small side canyon, go over a crest and begin descending. The several paths you've passed are the abandoned remains of earlier volunteer trail building efforts.

Cross a small side stream then pass an area of interesting, large rock outcroppings. Several hundred feet beyond the outcroppings ford a small stream at the base of a tall, whispy waterfall. Climb moderately to a large rocky slope, reenter woods, cross a smaller rocky area and continue through forest to the junction of the Herman Bridge Trail No. 406-E (see No. 26).

Keep left and wind down to the bridge over Herman Creek then climb in one switchback. Where you meet an old road, parallel it on the left then walk along the bed. Resume hiking up a trail then keep left at the junction of the connector to Trail No's. 27 through 30 and continue downhill to the Columbia Gorge Work Center. To date, this is the easternmost extent of No. 400, the Gorge Trail.

The Pinnacles

Trail Head

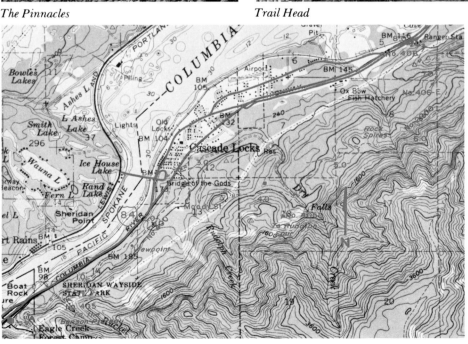

23 RUCKEL CREEK TRAIL

One day trip
Distance: 4 miles one way
Elevation gain: 3,800 feet; loss 200 feet
High Point: 3,700 feet
Allow 3 hours one way
Usually open mid-April through November
Topographic map:
 U.S.G.S. Bonneville Dam, Oreg.-Wash.
 15' **1957**

During late April the two huge hanging meadows traversed midway along the Ruckel Creek Trail support the most impressive wildflower displays in the Columbia Gorge. But even at other times of the hiking year, this route is an exceptionally scenic trip with lovely woods, viewpoints and a large basin of lichen-covered rocks and Indian pits, the likes of which are seen no where else in the Gorge. The trip can be done as a fun, but demanding, loop by combining it with the Ruckel Ridge Trail (No. 24). No additional mileage would be added and the loop is best made by doing Ruckel Ridge first.

From the west drive on I-84 to the Eagle Creek Park Exit 41, turn right at the end of the exit, drive 100 feet to a parking area where the road forks and leave your car here. To return westbound after the hike, continue 1.4 miles east on I-84 to the Cascade Locks exit. Approaching from the east, take I-84 to the Bonneville Dam Interchange, Exit 40, then head east 1.2 miles to the Eagle Creek Park exit.

Walk northeast up the paved road to the campground for 75 yards to a sign on the left shoulder identifying the Gorge Trail No. 400. Wind up above the fish hatchery to the edge of a bluff over the freeway. Turn right and follow along the fence to the north end of the campground and the junction of the trail to Buck Point and Ruckel Ridge. Keep left and descend to a large clearing. Follow the trail across the meadow to a section of the Old Columbia River Highway and walk along it for several hundred feet to Ruckel Creek. The trail proper resumes just beyond the east end of the ornate bridge over the stream, the last dependable source of water along the trail until 4.0 miles. The route of Trail No. 22 continues along the road bed.

Travel beside Ruckel Creek for several yards then switchback four times and come to an open area around a power line tower. Ruckel Ridge is directly to the south and is visible during most of the climb. Switchback five more times to the edge of a large rocky bowl. Descend into it and pass several Indian pits just off the trail. Anthropologists do not know whether these were built for pragmatic or ritualistic reasons.

Reenter woods and switchback twice then wind up on or near the crest of a narrow ridge. Traverse for a considerable distance before switchbacking nine times to a very exposed viewpoint at the tenth turn where you can see Mounts Adams and St. Helens, the Columbia River and the Bridge of the Gods. Make two more sets of switchbacks then abruptly leave the coniferous woods at a crest of grass and oaks. Curve left and traverse an open slope to a second, similarly vegetated crest where you can see Mt. Hood and Indian Mountain. Traverse two meadows separated by a finger of evergreens then continue at a gradual grade to the largest of the hanging meadows at 2.4 miles.

At the east end of the expanse resume traveling in woods and switchback four times. Traverse to a small open slope then begin climbing at an erratic, but moderately steep, grade 100 feet above Ruckel Creek. Near 3.8 miles cross a rocky slope and continue winding up through woods. Level off and pass the junction on your left of the trail to Rudolph Spur that descends to the Eagle-Herman Creek Traverse Trail (No. 22). One hundred fifty yards farther along the main trail come to the possibly signed and flagged route west to Ruckel Ridge. Head downhill, following the occasional blazes and tags, for a few hundred yards to a cool spot beside Ruckel Creek. The main route continues northeast another 1.5 miles to the Pacific Crest Trail on the east edge of the Benson Plateau (No. 26).

Bridge of the Gods from viewpoint

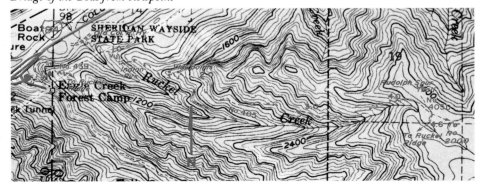

24 RUCKEL RIDGE

One day trip
Distance: 3.8 miles one way
Elevation gain: 3,700 feet; loss 100 feet
High Point: 3,700 feet
Allow 3 hours one way
Usually open late May through November
Topographic map:
  U.S.G.S. Bonneville Dam, Oreg.-Wash.
  15'   1957

Although Ruckel Ridge is a favorite conditioning hike of mountaineers, the climb is an outstanding trip for anyone who doesn't mind some steep grades and exposure. If you plan to follow Ruckel Ridge for its entire length to the Benson Plateau, you are encouraged to return along the Ruckel Creek Trail (No. 23), one of the most spectacular routes in the Gorge. Carry water as none is available until 3.8 miles.

From the west proceed on I-84 to the Eagle Creek Park Exit. Turn right at the end of the exit, drive 100 feet to a parking area where the road forks and leave your car here. To return westbound after the hike, drive 1.4 miles east to the Cascade Locks exit. Approaching from the east, take I-84 to the Bonneville Dam Interchange, Exit 40, then head east 1.2 miles to the Eagle Creek Park exit.

Walk northeast up the paved road to the campground for 75 yards to a sign on the left shoulder identifying the Gorge Trail No. 400. Wind up to the edge of a bluff above the

freeway, turn right and follow along the fence to the north end of the campground and the junction of the route to Ruckel Creek Trail. Turn right, following the sign pointing to Buck Point, and go along the edge of the camping area to its other (northeast) side where a sign near campsites 5 and 6 states *Buck Point Trail.* Climb at a moderate grade in six switchbacks then come to a large boulder on the right side of the trail and turn left onto the unmarked path across from the rock. The main route continues a few hundred yards to Buck Point. Make six short switchbacks up to a viewpoint at a cleared swath under a power line tower.

Reenter woods then descend slightly before traversing a slope of lichen-covered rocks. After a few hundred feet be watching for a switchback up to the left and follow it. Continue over small boulders and slabs in a northerly direction to the open, small, relatively flat crest at the north end of the ridge just above the line of fir trees. Turn right and walk southeast up the crest several yards to the bottom of the cliff face. Turn left and follow along the base of the wall then curve right and begin climbing very steeply along the east side of the ridge to its narrow crest. Although the remainder of the hike is mostly along a ridge crest only a few yards wide, and in a few places considerably narrower, the climb is never tedious.

At 2.5 miles come to the only serious impediment on the hike, a section of dangerously narrow and exposed outcroppings. Circumvent this by following a path that heads steeply down the south (right) side a few yards before the "Catwalk." Scramble along the faint detour back to the crest then several hundred feet farther come to a large, open rocky face, curve right and traverse across it. Continue around the south side of the slope, reenter woods and soon begin descending to a saddle.

From the saddle, follow the path along the left (north) slope and then climb steeply to the ridge top. Eventually, the crest broadens and the trail winds up very steeply to the edge of the Benson Plateau where the grade abruptly levels off. Follow tree blazes in a northeasterly direction for 0.3 mile until you reach Ruckel Creek. This level stretch also may be tagged. If you're making the loop, ford the stream and head gradually uphill to the northeast (left) at about an 30° angle to the stream until you intersect the Ruckel Creek Trail and turn left.

Hikers on Ruckel Ridge Trail

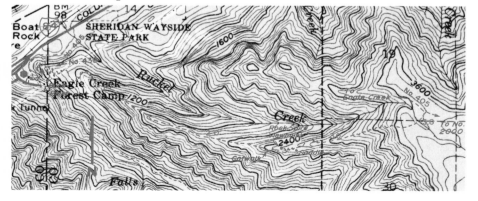

25 EAGLE CREEK TRAIL to WAHTUM LAKE

Backpack
Distance: 14 miles one way
Elevation gain: 3,840 feet
High Point: 3,950 feet
Allow 8 to 10 hours one way
Usually open June through November
Topographic map:
U.S.G.S. Bonneville Dam, Oreg.-Wash.
15'   **1957**

The Columbia Gorge is blessed with un-counted waterfalls, lovely streams and spec-tacular cliffs. The special lure of the Eagle Creek Trail is that it has all these attributes plus many of its own, such as the deep pool of the Punch Bowl at 2.1 miles and a 25-foot long tunnel that has been blasted out behind a falls at 6.0 miles. Since over three-quarters of the elevation gain is beyond Tunnel Falls, you can enjoy most of the scenic highlights of the trip without excessive climbing. Because of a few exposed sections, this is not a good hike for young children.

Those hiking all the way to Wahtum Lake could establish a car shuttle and do the trip one way or they could return along the Benson Plateau (No. 26) or Herman Creek (No. 28) Trails. You could make a scenic loop without needing a car shuttle by following the Ruckel Creek Trail No. 405 (No. 23) down from the Benson Plateau.

Since the Eagle Creek Trail is one of the most heavily used routes in the Gorge, hikers are asked to leave their dogs at home. Also camping before the 7.0 mile point is allowed at only four sites: Tenas Camp, 3.7 miles; Wy'east Camp, 4.7 miles; Blue Grouse Camp, 5.3 miles and 7½ Mile Camp at 7.0 miles. Backpackers should use portable stoves, not build wood fires.

From the west drive on I-84 to the Eagle Creek Park Exit 41, and turn right at the end of the exit. After 100 feet keep right at a fork and continue 0.5 mile along the narrow paved road to its end at a large turnaround. To return westbound after the hike, continue 1.4 miles east on I-84 to the Cascade Locks exit. Approaching from the east, take I-84 to the Bonneville Dam Interchange, Exit 40, then head east 1.2 miles to the Eagle Creek Park exit.

Walk along the steep, wooded slope above Eagle Creek along a trail that is paved for the first 0.3 mile and after 0.7 mile traverse a sheer rock wall several hundred feet above the stream. Continue along somewhat less precipitous slopes, traveling through woods and occasional small grassy patches. At 1.5 miles a short side loop descends to a view of Metlako Falls. Cross Sorenson Creek, tra-verse out of the side canyon formed by the stream and pass a sign identifying a 0.2 mile spur down to creek level just below the Punch Bowl. A short distance farther the main trail comes to a viewpoint 100 feet above Punch-bowl Falls and the pool.

Cross Tish Creek and an unnamed side stream on bridges and at 3.0 miles travel above a narrow gorge of vertical walls. At its southern end cross the 80-foot chasm on High Bridge. After 0.7 mile recross Eagle Creek on a bridge and continue traversing through woods. Cross Wy'east Creek and another side stream on log spans and near 5.3 miles pass the junction of the Eagle-Benson Way Trail. You can make a fun, but hard, loop by following this steep route up to Camp Smokey on the Benson Plateau then heading north 1.4 miles to the Ruckel Creek Trail. The entire circuit would involve 15.2 miles and 4,200 feet of uphill.

Traverse a scree slope and travel in and out of the steep-sided canyon holding Tunnel Falls. Pass just above an impressive falls on Eagle Creek then walk close to the stream. If you're making a one day hike, the rocky bank between the trail and the flow is a good place for lunch before you return.

Continue parallel to Eagle Creek, cross two side streams and at 7.6 miles come to the junction of the Eagle-Tanner Trail to Tanner Butte. Turn sharply left and climb through woods. Recross the two streams you forded before the switchback and at 9.3 miles come to Inspiration Point and a fine view over lower Eagle Creek gorge. Turn right and traverse through deep woods for 0.5 mile to the junc-tion of the Indian Springs Trail. Stay left and continue traversing uphill to Wahtum Lake. To make any of the possible long loops follow the Pacific Crest Trail No. 2000 around the south and east slope of the bowl holding the lake.

High Bridge on upper Eagle Creek

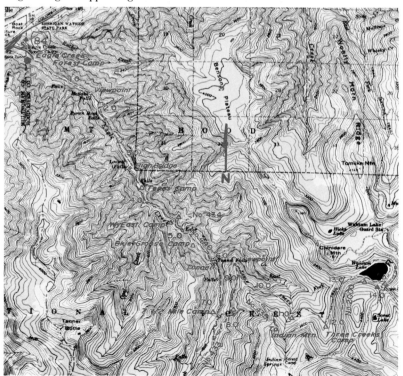

26 BENSON PLATEAU

Backpack
Distance: 14 miles one way
Elevation gain: 4,940 feet; loss 930 feet
High Point: 4,200 feet
Allow 8 to 9 hours one way
Usually open June through November
Topographic map:
U.S.G.S. Bonneville Dam, Oreg.-Wash.
15'   1957

After winding up to the rim of a 3,600 foot wall this hike crosses the two mile long Benson Plateau near its eastern edge then follows a narrow ridge with many exceptional viewpoints to Wahtum Lake. Long loops could be made by returning along the Herman Creek Trail (No. 28) or, by establishing a short car shuttle, the Eagle Creek Trail (No. 25), the Ruckel Creek Trail (No. 23) or the Eagle-Benson Way No. 434 (see No. 25). The Benson Plateau itself is a maze of interconnecting trails that provide shorter variations. Carry water as few sources are available along Trail No. 2000.

From the west proceed on I-84 about 43 miles east of Portland to the Cascade Locks exit. Continue through the community to its east end then keep left where a sign marks the road to Industrial Park and Airport. Stay on this road for 2.0 miles, cross over the freeway, turn left at the end of the over-pass and drive 0.2 mile to the large parking area with a sign stating *Pacific Crest Trail*. Coming from the east, take the Forest Lane-Herman Creek exit between the 48 and 47 mileposts. After going under the freeway turn right and travel west 0.6 mile.

Climb several yards from a large wooden sign, cross the corner of the work center and rise in several switchbacks to a road. Cross it, walk along the slope then make one set of switchbacks up to the junction of the route to Trail No's. 27 through 30.

Keep right on the Herman Bridge Trail, descend then walk along an old road. Resume traveling on a trail and drop to the bridge across Herman Creek. Wind up to the junc-tion of the Pacific Crest Trail No. 2000 that begins its Oregon section at the Bridge of the Gods in Cascade Locks (see No. 22). Turn left, cross a scree slope and reenter woods. Make two sets of switchbacks, traverse and cross to the west side of the slope. Climb in irregular switchbacks for 1.0 mile then con-tinue uphill along a ridge crest. Pass a helispot and a good rest stop at 5.0 miles and keep climbing to the northeastern edge of the Benson Plateau.

Travel almost on the level and at 6.8 miles pass the northern end of Benson Way No. 405-B that meets the Ruckel Creek Trail at Hunters Camp. Water is available there and at Benson Camp. Stay left on No. 2000 and continue on the level for 0.4 mile to the junc-tion of the Benson-Ruckel Trail No. 405-A. Again stay straight and walk 0.6 mile to the eastern end of the Ruckel Creek Trail No. 405. Trail No. 2000 rises slightly then levels off. Just beyond where you leave the woods you will have a fine view of Mt. Hood. Con-tinue on the level through an area of small trees and dense beargrass. Begin dropping and pass the southern end of Trail No. 405-B. Descend along the wooded east side of the ridge for 0.2 mile to Camp Smokey and the junction of the Eagle-Benson Trail No. 434 to the Eagle Creek Trail.

Continue along the wooded slope at an er-ratic, but always gentle, grade then at 9.9 miles contour along a large scree slope where you'll have views of Mt. Adams, Tomlike Mountain and the valley holding the West Fork of Herman Creek. Cross to the west side of the ridge and traverse up through the re-mains of a burn that occurred in 1972. As you travel farther you'll have good views to the south and west, including Indian Mountain, Tanner Butte, the upper Eagle Creek valley and Mt. Hood.

Make one set of short switchbacks and 100 feet beyond the second turn pass a 75-foot long spur to a viewpoint. Continue uphill along the west side, passing a large sign at the faint junction of the obscure path to Hicks Lake. Rise at a gradual grade through in-creasingly open terrain that is a flower garden during early July. Just a few yards beyond where you reenter woods pass the 0.5 mile long spur to the summit of Mt. Chinindere. Seventy-five feet farther stay on No. 2000 at a sign and a few hundred feet beyond come to the junction of the 0.2 mile connector to Road N-20. The Pacific Crest Trail heads gradually downhill for 1.0 mile to Wahtum Lake.

Beargrass on Benson Plateau

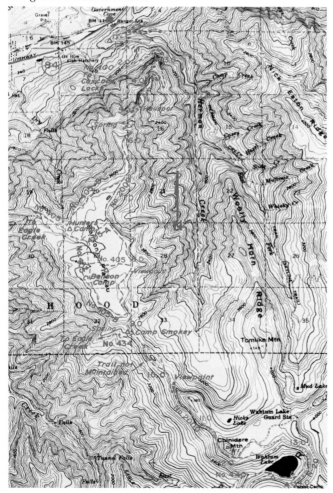

27 NICK EATON RIDGE

One day trip
Distance: 4.4 miles one way
Elevation gain: 4,080 feet; loss 100 feet
High Point: 4,100 feet
Allow 3 to 3½ hours one way
Usually open late May through November
Topographic map:
U.S.G.S. Bonneville Dam, Oreg.-Wash.
15'   1957

From the several open slopes on the west side of Nick Eaton Ridge you can look over the Herman Creek drainage, across to the Benson Plateau and west down the Columbia River. Combining this hike with the Gorton Creek Trail (No. 29) or a section of the Green Point Mountain-Casey Creek Loop (No. 30) creates a perfect loop trip. If you're making one of these circuits, it's more scenic to return along the Nick Eaton Trail. No drinking water is available along the Nick Eaton Trail.

Approaching from the west, proceed on I-84 about 43 miles from Portland to the Cascade Locks exit. Go through the community to its east end then keep left where a sign marks the road to Industrial Park and Airport. Stay on this road for 2.0 miles, cross over the freeway, turn left at the end of the overpass and drive 0.2 mile to a sign stating *Pacific Crest Trail* and a large parking area below the Columbia Gorge Work Center. Coming from

the east, take the Forest Lane-Herman Creek exit between the 48 and 47 mileposts then head west 0.6 mile along Forest Lane to the Work Center. The trail begins from the large wooden sign near the center of the parking area.

Climb a bank, cross the corner of the parking area for the work center to the resumption of the trail and wind up in several switchbacks to a road. Cross it, walk under power lines and travel past an area of boulders. Curve around the face of a slope, climb in one set of switchbacks and come to the junction of the Herman Bridge Trail to the Benson Plateau (No. 26). Keep left and traverse almost on the level to a dirt road.

Stay right and climb along the bed then level off and about 0.5 mile from where you met the road pass Herman Camp and the junction of the Gorton Creek Trail. Continue along the road about 250 yards to a sign on your left marking the beginning of the Nick Eaton Trail. The road continues to the beginning of the Herman Creek Trail (see No's. 28 and 30).

Meander up through attractive woods then begin switchbacking. Continue up across two small open areas, separated by woods, to a third, considerably larger break with extensive views to the west. These clearings are smothered with wildflowers about mid-May. Make six short switchbacks then reenter woods and wind up to the junction at 2.9 miles of the 0.5 mile Ridge Cutoff Trail No. 437 to the Gorton Creek Trail.

Keep straight (right) and after several yards come to a large open slope where you'll have a good view of the north face of Mt. Hood. On a warm, sunny day this is an enticing spot for a snack stop. Continue along the trail into woods then cross another open slope. The crest of the ridge, 150 feet above, affords good views. Reenter woods, switchback downhill once and descend briefly to a saddle. Walk along the crest with a few minor ups and downs to the junction of the Deadwood Trail No. 422 that drops for 0.7 mile before meeting the Gorton Creek Trail near a stream.

Stay right (straight) on the main route and climb along the ridge top. Where the crest broadens, keep left and rise along the east slope. Return to the crest and continue winding steeply up. Rise along it to an outcropping of rocks that is an appropriate place to end the trip if you're not making one of the possible loops.

Winter sunset on Benson Plateau

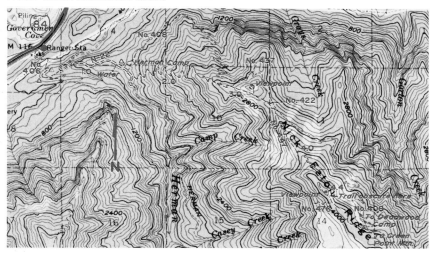

28 HERMAN CREEK TRAIL

Backpack
Distance: 12 miles one way
Elevation gain: 3,835 feet
High Point: 3,950 feet
Allow 6 to 7 hours one way
Usually open June through November
Topographic map:
   U.S.G.S. Bonneville Dam, Oreg.-Wash.
   15'   1957

The Herman Creek Trail, as with so many trips in the Gorge, can be combined with other routes to make various combinations of loops. If you're doing this hike, which traverses the length of a lushy wooded canyon, as a one day outing or want a shorter backpack and enjoy circuits, refer to Trail No. 30 for several possibilities. For a two to three day backpack you could return along the Benson Plateau (No. 26) or establish a short car shuttle and follow the Eagle Creek Trail (No. 25) back. You also could set up a long car shuttle and do the trip one way.

Approaching from the west, drive on I-84 about 43 miles from Portland to the Cascade Locks exit. Go through the community to its east end then keep left where a sign marks the road to Industrial Park and Airport. Stay on this road for 2.0 miles, cross over the freeway, then turn left at the end of the overpass and drive 0.2 mile to a sign stating *Pacific Crest Trail* and a large parking area below the Columbia Gorge Work Center. Coming from the east, take the Forest Lane-Herman Creek exit between the 48 and 47 mileposts then head west 0.6 mile along Forest Lane to the

Work Center. The trail begins from the large wooden sign near the center of the parking area.

Climb several yards along a bank, cross the corner of the parking area for the work center to the resumption of the trail and rise in several switchbacks of irregular length to a road. Cross it, walk under power lines and travel past an area of boulders. Curve around the face of a slope, climb in one set of switchbacks and come to the junction of the Herman Bridge Trail to the Benson Plateau.

Keep left, traverse 200 yards to an open area and cross it. Stay right on the road, climb, then level off and pass the beginning of the Gorton Creek Trail (No. 29) at Herman Camp. Continue along the road, passing the start of the Nick Eaton Trail (No. 27) after 250 yards, and stay on the road to its end at the beginning of the Herman Creek Trail.

Descend past two waterfalls, then climb to the deep, narrow side canyon holding Camp Creek. Ford the stream, traverse out, and descend to a third waterfall. Soon resume climbing to the junction of the Casey Creek Trail No. 476, just before a campsite. A spur from the west edge of the clearing descends for 0.4 mile to the confluence of the East and West Forks of Herman Creek.

Continue south on the level along Trail No. 406 and then begin climbing steadily. Along the next two miles make easy crossings of three large streams and five smaller ones. At 7.0 miles come to the junction of the Herman Creek Cutoff No. 410 to Road N-20 and to the southern end of the Gorton Creek Trail.

Keep straight (right) and after a few yards pass Cedar Swamp Shelter. Water is available a short distance farther along the trail. Ford the East Fork of Herman Creek and pass 7½ Mile Camp.

Resume climbing along increasingly open slopes, switchback a few times and at 8.3 miles come to the junction of the short spur to Mud Lake. Keep right (straight) and traverse a mostly treeless area low on the southeastern shoulder of Tomlike Mountain. Switchback to the top of the ridge where a spur heads north for 1.0 mile with 500 feet of elevation gain to Tomlike Mountain. Stay left on the main trail and several yards farther come to the junction of the Anthill Trail. It climbs for 0.5 mile to Road N-20 and the route to the right joins the road farther to the west. If you're making one of the long loops, follow the latter then walk along Road N-20 for 0.4 mile to a spur of the Benson Plateau Trail.

Cedar Swamp Shelter

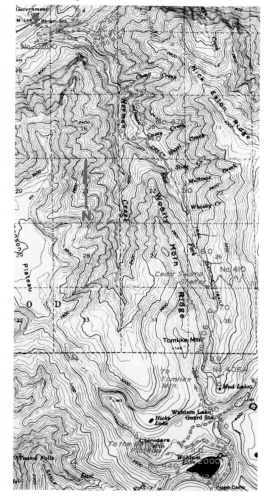

29 GORTON CREEK TRAIL

One day trip
Distance: 6.2 miles one way
Elevation gain: 4,180 feet; loss 200 feet
High Point: 4,100 feet
Allow 4 hours one way
Usually open June through October
Topographic map:
U.S.G.S. Bonneville Dam, Oreg.-Wash.
15'   1957

As with many landmarks in the Gorge, Gorton Creek was named for a homesteader. However, Edwin Gorton, who settled there in the 1890's, was a relative latecomer to the area compared with those who had established homes and businesses as early as the 1850's.

The Gorton Creek Trail that, by the way, is never near its namesake can be done as three scenic loops of varying lengths by following the connectors No. 437 or No. 422 to the Nick Eaton Trail (No. 27) or, most demanding, taking the Gorton Creek Trail all the way up to the crest of Nick Eaton Ridge and returning along the Nick Eaton Trail or the Casey Creek Trail (No. 30). Easily accessible water is not available until 3.9 miles along the Gorton Creek Trail.

Approaching from the west, proceed on I-84 about 43 miles from Portland to the Cascade Locks exit. Go through the community to its east end then keep left where a sign marks the road to Industrial Park and Airport. Stay on this road for 2.0 miles, cross over the freeway, turn left at the end of the overpass and drive 0.2 mile to a sign stating *Pacific Crest Trail* and a large parking area below the Columbia Gorge Work Center. Coming from the east, take the Forest Lane-Herman Creek exit between the 48 and 47 mileposts then head west 0.6 mile along Forest Lane to the Work Center. The trail begins from the large wooden sign near the center of the parking area.

Climb up a bank, cross the corner of the parking area for the work center to the resumption of the trail and climb in several switchbacks for 0.3 mile to a road. Cross it, walk under power lines and travel past an area of boulders. Curve around the face of a slope and switchback up to the junction of the Herman Bridge Trail to the Benson Plateau (No. 26). Keep left, traverse almost on the level for 200 yards to an open area and cross it in the same direction you were heading.

Stay right and climb along a road, level off and at 1.4 miles turn left into the clearing at Herman Camp. The main road continues southeast, past the Nick Eaton Trail, to the Herman Creek Trail (No. 28).

Walk northeast from the clearing at Herman Camp along an old road and begin climbing moderately steeply. The bed eventually narrows to a trail that has a more reasonable grade. Climb in three sets of switchbacks separated by traverses then near 2.7 miles cross over the crest of a slope, re-cross the face in a switchback and make a long traverse to the south. Switchback and continue across another ridge face, traverse to a third one, make two short switchbacks and come to a fourth and then the junction of Trail No. 437.

Keep striaght (left) and begin descending gradually. Seventy-five feet from the junction pass two decomposing stumps on your left where an unsigned path drops steeply for 0.2 mile, losing several hundred feet of elevation, to the spectacular rock pinnacle called Indian Point. Continue descending along the main trail and a few yards beyond where the route curves right at 3.9 miles come to the junction of No. 422. Turn left, cross a stream and climb above Deadwood Camp, a good place to end the hike if you don't want to make the climb to the ridge crest.

The trail climbs at a moderately steep grade in several short switchbacks to a view of Mt. Defiance (No. 33) and Dog Mountain (No. 3). Hike up along the crest then climb at a consistently steep angle. Leave the ridge top and traverse gradually down along the east slope where you'll have more extensive views. Continue mostly downhill, cross a small stream, the last source of water, then wind down at a steeper grade for a short distance. Resume climbing steeply, make two short switchbacks and continue uphill. A level stretch offers a brief respite before the final climb to the crest and a junction. To make either of the long loops, turn right.

Indian Point

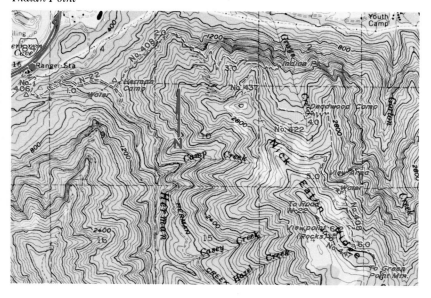

30 GREEN POINT MOUNTAIN-CASEY CREEK LOOP

One day trip (long) or backpack
Distance: 19 miles round trip
Elevation gain: 4,750 feet
High Point: 4,736 feet
Allow 9 to 10 hours round trip
Usually open June through November
Topographic map:
U.S.G.S. Bonneville Dam, Oreg.-Wash.
15'   1957

If the entire Green Point Mountain-Casey Creek Loop, a most interesting but little used circuit, takes more time and energy than you have, one considerably shorter variation would be to follow No. 476 at 3.9 miles to the Nick Eaton Trail No. 447 (No. 27) and return along that scenic route. By studying the map you can create many other combinations and permutations on the basic loop.

From the west, proceed on I-84 about 43 miles east of Portland to the Cascade Locks exit. Continue through the community to its east end then keep left where a sign marks the road to Industrial Park and Airport. Stay on this road for 2.0 miles, cross over the freeway, turn left at the end of the overpass and drive 0.2 mile to a sign stating *Pacific Crest Trail* and a large parking area. Coming from the east, take the Forest Lane-Herman Creek exit between the 48 and 47 mileposts then head west 0.6 mile along Forest Lane to the parking area. The trail begins from the large wooden sign near the center of the turnouts.

Climb several yards, cross the corner of the parking area for the work center to the resumption of the trail and switchback up to a road. Cross it, travel at a gradual grade then climb in one set of switchbacks to the junction of the Herman Bridge Trail to the Benson Plateau (No. 26).

Keep left, walk on the level for 200 yards to a flat, open area and cross it in the same direction you were heading. Keep right and climb along a road for 0.4 mile then level off. Pass the beginning of the Gorton Creek Trail (No. 29), and 250 yards farther come to the start of the Nick Eaton Trail. Continue along the road to its end at the Herman Creek Trail.

Descend along the east wall of the huge valley, pass a tall thin waterfall and continue downhill to the base of an even larger cascade. Begin climbing and eventually level off and hike into the deep narrow side canyon holding Camp Creek. Ford the flow, traverse out the opposite side and descend to a third waterfall. Soon resume climbing and come to the junction of the Casey Creek Trail No. 476 just before a campsite at a clearing. A spur from the west edge of the clearing descends for 0.4 mile to the confluence of the East and West Forks of Herman Creek.

Continue on No. 406 and after a short level stretch begin climbing steadily. Along the next two miles make easy crossings of three large streams and five smaller ones. At 7.0 miles come to the junction of the Herman Creek Cutoff No. 410 and Cedar Swamp Shelter. Turn left onto Trail No. 410, walk on the level to a stream crossing, the last good source of water, and soon begin climbing. Pass through a swampy area then continue traversing and switchbacking uphill. Near 9.0 miles level off, pass a small structure and several yards beyond it come to Road N-20. Follow Trail No. 408, the Gorton Creek Trail, that heads north from the road. Walk on the level for 100 yards then climb to the summit of Green Point Mountain where you'll have extensive views.

To make the loop, continue heading north near the edge of the open slope then begin descending in woods. At the junction of the Green Point Ridge Trail No. 418 keep left and travel gradually downhill for 1.5 miles to the junction of the Plateau Cutoff Trail No. 412 to the Green Point Ridge Trail. Keep left again and switchback down steeply. Come to a sign stating *Ridge Camp* and a tagged path heading east to water. Continue in more open terrain along the eastern side of the ridge. Come to a junction and turn left onto Nick Eaton Way. Climb briefly then travel near the crest for 0.3 mile to the junction of the Casey Creek Trail. Turn left and begin descending along a steep, narrow trail. Traverse through a more open, brushy section, resume dropping steeply, pass through a delightful grassy area then reenter woods and switchback and traverse down to the junction with the Herman Creek Trail.

Mount Defiance from Green Point Mountain

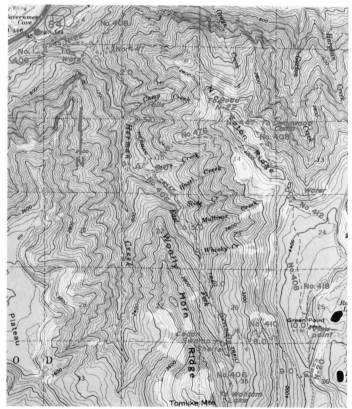

31 WYETH TRAIL

One day trip or backpack
Distance: 5.5 miles one way
Elevation gain: 3,930 feet
High Point: 4,070 feet
Allow 4 hours one way
Usually open late May through November
Topographic map:
   U.S.G.S. Bonneville Dam, Oreg.-Wash.
   15'   **1957**

Although steep along many stretches, the Wyeth Trail to North Lake is a popular trip with backpackers as well as hikers wanting a reasonably short, but strenuous, outing. The route winds through some of the loveliest woods in the Columbia Gorge and also traverses many clearings that afford views of Mounts Adams, St. Helens and Defiance (No. 33), Wind and Dog (No. 3) Mountains and the fertile farmlands of the Carson Valley.

If reaching North Lake's shore isn't demanding enough, you could continue another 1.1 miles and climb 200 feet to Rainy Lake just off Road N-20. Long loop trips involving car shuttles are possible by following seldom used routes east from North Lake to Mt. Defiance or south from the junction at 4.0 miles to Green Point Mountain (No. 30).

Drive on I-84 to the Wyeth Interchange near milepost 51. Turn right at the end of the exit if you're coming from the west or go under the freeway if you're approaching from the east and proceed several yards to a junction. Turn right and drive west 50 yards to an unpaved road on your left that is marked by a somewhat obscure sign stating *Wyeth Trail*. Turn sharply left and go 0.1 mile

to a parking area across from a sign identifying the trailhead.

Walk on the level, cross a cleared area under power lines then reenter woods and ford a small stream. At 0.3 mile pass an unmarked path on your left that goes to private property. Wind up at an increasingly steep grade through the attractive forest of widely-spaced conifers and large, but delicate, vine maple. Traverse a rocky slope three times at successively higher angles. From these clear areas you can see down to the Columbia River and over a bucolic scene along Herman Creek Road.

Continue steeply uphill to the edge of the canyon holding Harphan Creek. The pinnacle jutting up from the north face of the ridge to the west is Indian Point (see No. 29). Climb moderately along the eastern wall below an area of exceptionally tall and dense vine maple. Traverse at a gradual grade, with even a short downhill stretch, and come to the edge of the canyon a second time. Climb very steeply for a short distance to a stream crossing at 2.0 miles.

Continue steeply up near the stream, make a few short switchbacks and come, again, to the canyon's edge. Travel along the crest of a narrow ridge then wind up in several short switchbacks to a rocky area that offers a fine view across the Columbia River to the Carson Valley and beyond. Wind up to the top of the open area and resume climbing steeply in woods, just skirting the western edge of a rocky swath. Travel at a more moderate grade along a brushy area then rise steeply along an open slope. Reenter forest, climb in eight switchbacks and after a level stretch come to the junction of the Green Point Ridge Trail No. 418 at 4.0 miles.

Keep left and traverse. Soon you'll have views of tower-topped Mt. Defiance, the highest point in the Columbia Gorge. Descend to a small level area that is swampy early in the hiking season, continue downhill and cross a stream. Begin climbing and pass a brushy clearing on your left. Hike steadily uphill, cross two small streams and come to an unsigned junction. Turn right and walk 30 yards to the earth dam at North Lake. This fill is the scurrying ground for a dense chipmunk population.

To visit Rainy Lake or Mt. Defiance, head south from the unsigned junction just before North Lake for 75 yards to a junction and turn right to reach the former or left for the latter.

North Lake

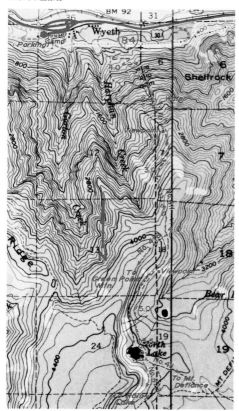

32 SHELLROCK MOUNTAIN

One-half day trip
Distance: 1.3 miles one way
Elevation gain: 1,200 feet
High Point: 1,300 feet
Allow 1 hour one way
Usually open February through December
Topographic map:
   U.S.G.S. Hood River, Oreg.-Wash.
   15'   **1957**

Shellrock Mountain is across the Columbia River from Wind Mountain and its route begins directly from I-84. In fact, you can see the first mile of trail methodically switchbacking up the scree as you drive past on the freeway. Three short side trips, one to a steep, grassy viewpoint and two along an interesting old road, are possible added attractions. Since most of the trail is rocky, your feet will appreciate sturdy hiking boots. No water is available along this route.

From the west, proceed on I-84 just beyond the east end of a high steel retaining wall above the freeway about midway between the 52 and 53 mileposts to where a small turnout at a segment of the Old Highway provides space for parking. To return west after the hike, you'll have to travel east 3.7 miles to the Viento Park Interchange. If you're approaching from the east, go to the Wyeth Interchange near the 51 milepost then head east 1.6 miles to the trailhead.

Walk east along the old road bed for 75 yards then take a faint path that heads from the right shoulder through rocks. After several feet curve left and traverse up to the east along an obvious tread. Climb more steeply in six short switchbacks to the old wagon road, paved now with a spongy cushion of moss. For short side trips you can walk both directions along the road. The eastern segment ends after a few hundred yards at a deep gully caused by stream erosion and the longer, western section disappears into a rock slide above the freeway after several hundred yards.

To continue the hike, walk east along a treeless section of the old road about 75 yards to the edge of the woods where a trail climbs the rocky slope. At the second switchback a side path heads east to a steep grassy perch below the power lines. Switchback nine more times along the main trail, enjoying good views to the east as you rise higher. Enter sparse woods and switchback four times, mostly along a northeast facing slope. Make a long traverse to the south then switchback a final time and travel north and west to a clearing. The small structure several yards downslope is an observation station built by the U.S. Geological Survey for monitoring possible land slippage in the Wind Mountain area across the Columbia River.

The summit of Shellrock Mountain is 800 feet higher. Apparently, a trail never was constructed beyond 1.5 miles and reaching the top would involve considerable bushwhacking.

Wagon road on Shellrock Mountain

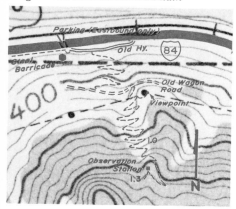

33 MT. DEFIANCE

One day trip
Distance: 6 miles one way
Elevation gain: 4,815 feet
High Point: 4,960 feet
Allow 4 to 5 hours one way
Usually open June through October
Topographic map:
 U.S.G.S. Hood River, Oreg.-Wash.
 15'   1957

Mt. Defiance is the highest point in the Columbia Gorge and, like Ruckel Ridge (No. 24), is a popular conditioning trip for mountaineers. The hike can be done as a rigorously fun loop by combining it with the newly reopened Starvation Ridge Trail (No. 34). This circuit would add no distance and, if you plan to make it, preferably follow the Starvation Ridge Trail going up.

From the west drive on I-84 about 55 miles from Portland to the Starvation Creek Rest Area and park in one of the turnouts. To return westbound after the hike, you'll have to head east 0.7 mile to the Viento Park Interchange. If you're approaching from the east, travel on I-84 to the Wyeth Interchange near milepost 51 then proceed east 4.0 miles to the Starvation Creek Rest Area.

Walk west back along the entrance road to a sign stating Mt. Defiance Trail. Parallel the freeway on the south side of a cement barricade to a section of the Old Columbia River Highway. Follow the road past Cabin Creek Falls then begin hiking on a trail. Curve left into a clearing that is fast being overtaken by Scotch broom and ford Warren Creek below Hole-in-the-Wall Falls, a manmade diversion.

Traverse up for 200 yards to the junction of the Starvation Ridge No. 414, the route of the possible loop.

Keep right (straight) and continue traversing. Pass Lancaster Falls, the last easily accessible and plentiful source of water, then soon travel along a power line cut to a sign at the faint junction of the original route of the trail. Keep left and soon begin a series of short switchbacks. Traverse the east facing slope of a side canyon to a sign identifying the 100 foot long spur to water, the last available on the hike. Climb more steeply in short switchbacks and traverses to the edge of Lindsey Creek canyon. Walk on the level for several yards across an old logging road then traverse a slope of grass, trees and, in spring, wildflowers, before resuming switchbacking.

Pass a second viewpoint at the edge of the canyon and continue winding up the face of the ridge then near 2.8 miles come to its crest. Your leg muscles will enjoy the next 0.2 miles of level grade. Climb moderately along an old road then rise more steeply, mostly traversing but with a few short sections that head directly up the slope or switchback. Around 4.0 miles begin climbing through an area of smaller conifers near a ridge crest.

Leave the woods and wind up an open area near the edge of a steep, rocky slope then traverse to a level boulder field, another respite for your legs. Resume climbing moderately and come to the junction of the Mitchell Point Trail No. 417 that descends for 1.0 mile to Warren Lake, 600 feet below, and the upper end of the Starvation Ridge Trail.

Turn right and continue up for 0.1 mile to a switchback to the right. The faint trail heading straight here is the route of a little loop you could make on the return. Turn right and traverse at a gradual grade along the open slope. Curve to the south, travel briefly through woods then make a long traverse along a scree slope. Bear Lake is below and Green Point Mountain (No. 30) is the high point on the ridge above it. Have a fine view of Mt. Hood then come to the junction of Trail No. 413 to Bear Lake.

Turn left, switchback three times and head north over a faint tread to the summit. You'll see the major Cascade peaks from Mt. Hood north to Mt. Rainier plus the Upper and Lower Hood River Valleys, the Columbia River and other landmarks. To make the little loop, walk to the northeast end of the summit area and follow a trail down, crossing Road N-21 twice.

Bear Lake from Mt. Defiance

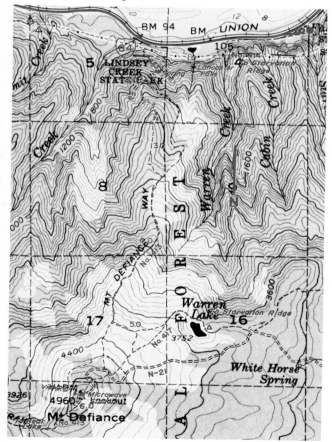

34 STARVATION RIDGE

One day trip
Distance: 6 miles one way
Elevation gain: 4,050 feet; loss 350 feet
High Point: 3,850 feet
Allow 3½ to 4 hours one way
Usually open June through October
Topographic map:
   U.S.G.S. Hood River, Oreg.-Wash.
   15'   1957

You don't have to go long distances to enjoy extensive views and fine scenery in the Columbia Gorge. On the hike up Starvation Ridge a level viewpoint at 1.4 miles is a perfect place to stop if you want a short trip or you could make a 2.5 mile loop by ending the climb at 1.8 miles and returning along No. 414B. A giant loop, that would add one mile and 600 feet of uphill, is possible by continuing above Warren Lake and returning along the Mt. Defiance Trail (No. 33).

From the west proceed on I-84 about 55 miles from Portland to the Starvation Creek Rest Area and park in one of the turnouts. To return westbound after the hike, you'll have to head east 0.7 mile to the Viento Park Interchange. If you're approaching from the east, travel on I-84 to the Wyeth Interchange near milepost 51 then drive east 4.0 miles to the Starvation Creek Rest Area.

Walk west back along the entrance road to a sign stating *Mt. Defiance Trail*. Parallel the freeway on the south side of a cement barricade to a section of the Old Columbia River Highway. Follow the bed past Cabin Creek Falls then begin hiking on a trail. Curve left into a clearing and ford Warren Creek below Hole-in-the-Wall Falls. Traverse up for 200 yards to the junction of the Starvation Ridge Trail No. 414. Trail No. 413 continues to Mt. Defiance.

Turn left and traverse steeply uphill. Curve into the side canyon holding Warren Creek and travel on the level to a ford of the stream. Switchback twice then cross an open grassy slope that is a flower garden around mid April. Switchback and go under power lines.

Switchback under the power lines again. Wind up in three turns to a small grove of oak, fir and bushes, switchback and come to a crest where you can see the flat viewpoint at 1.4 miles just ahead and below. Descend and pass the side path to the overlook. Continue downhill in four switchbacks to a lush side canyon and the ford of Cabin Creek, the last easily reached drinking water. Traverse to a signed junction where Trail No. 414B to the left (north) descends for 0.5 mile to the Old Columbia River Highway 0.2 mile west of the Rest Area. If you plan to take this cut-off on the return, note landmarks as a faint path farther along the main trail also heads north, but soon dead ends.

Keep right, wind up and go under a power line tower then continue switchbacking up to a ridge crest and another tower. Turn right, walk along the ridge top for several yards and enter woods. Climb mostly along the crest at a generally steep grade. Where you come to short stretches where the tread is faint, look for tags and stakes. Keep left at a possibly unsigned path that goes to water. Near 4.1 miles cross a small scree slope then reenter woods and begin a series of short switchbacks. Volunteer labor is responsible for reopening the Starvation Ridge Trail and before it was brushed out in 1977 this section was almost impassable. Traverse a larger scree area on a wide trail then travel through woods to an old logging road. Follow the bed for a few hundred feet then watch for tape on the right that marks the resumption of the trail.

Climb in four switchbacks and at 5.0 miles travel above a newer logging road and clear-cut. Hike uphill then walk on the level along a crest and come to a viewpoint. Continue on the level through open then wooded terrain to the junction of a route that goes 150 feet south to Road N-21. Turn right and descend gradually for 0.4 mile to Warren Lake.

To make the loop, head west at the junction 50 yards above the lake and walk around the north shore then wind up in a generally westerly direction along a sometimes faint tread to the Mt. Defiance Trail.

Columbia River from first viewpoint

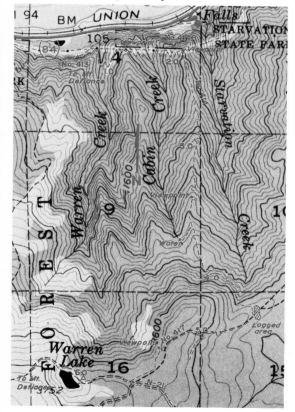

35 WYGANT TRAIL

One day trip
Distance: 4 miles one way
Elevation gain: 1,800 feet; loss 100 feet
High Point: 1,800 feet
Allow 2 to 2½ hours one way
Usually open March through November
Topographic map:
  U.S.G.S. Hood River, Oreg.-Wash.
  15'   1957

The circuitous Wygant Trail offers a mix of varied scenery including grassy slopes with gnarled, photogenic oak trees, evergreen woods the equal of those encountered farther west in the moister sections of the Gorge, rocky viewpoints affording especially good views to the east, and a section of the original Columbia River Highway. Except for a few short descents and level stretches, the trail climbs at a steady, moderate grade to a small clearing at the summit of a peak, an inviting place for a leisurely lunch.

From the west drive on I-84 2.5 miles beyond the Viento Park Interchange near milepost 56 to the next exit that is unsigned but leads to Lausman Picnic Area. Turn right at the end of the exit, as indicated by the sign stating *Parking for Wygant Trail*, and travel 0.2 mile along the old highway to its end. After the hike, you'll have to drive 3.6 miles east to the West Hood River Interchange, Exit 62.

Approaching from the east, proceed on I-84 to the Viento Park Interchange then travel east the 2.5 miles to the Lausman Park exit.

Hike up a dirt road that begins from the west end of the paved old highway for about 100 feet then keep right, following the sign pointing to Trail. Walk on the level, cross a stream in a small side canyon then descend gradually to another segment of the old highway. Walk west along the road for 0.3 mile to another sign identifying the resumption of the trail from the left (south) shoulder. Travel up a ravine and make four short switchbacks then follow an erratic, but gradual, grade to a junction at 1.0 mile. A spur goes right to a viewpoint above the freeway and the main trail heads left down along the oak covered wall of Perham Creek canyon to a single fat log with a railing over the stream. Perham Creek is the last source of water.

Go uphill about 100 feet and turn right where a path heads left toward the creek. Continue gradually uphill then walk on the level to an open, grassy viewpoint on a rock outcropping above the Columbia River. The trail almost doubles back from the overlook and after a few hundred feet crosses an old roadbed. Switchback and travel east along the cleared swath under power lines then curve right into a wooded side canyon. Climb in a series of short traverses and switchbacks, passing viewpoints in settings of grass and oaks at two of the turns. The rock mass to the east seen from the second viewpoint is Mitchell Point.

Make a long, gradual traverse to the west along the forested slope. Cross a small washout and continue traversing to a switchback where a path heads straight to an exposed viewpoint. Recross the washout, switchback and pass the slide a third time. Continue traversing, curve left into a side canyon then switchback three times and come to a viewpoint on a slope of grass and large, scattered conifers at the fourth turn.

For the next mile climb at a steady grade through woods in 15 switchbacks near the crest. Occasionally, the trail changes from the east to the west sides or comes to grassy clearings with views of Wind and Dog (No. 3) Mountains in Washington. Walk along the crest of an east-west oriented ridge at a gradual grade then make two short switchbacks and come to a small clearing that marks the end of the hike. Trees now block much of the view, but a fire lookout once occupied this site.

Hikers on trail

Bridge over Perham Creek

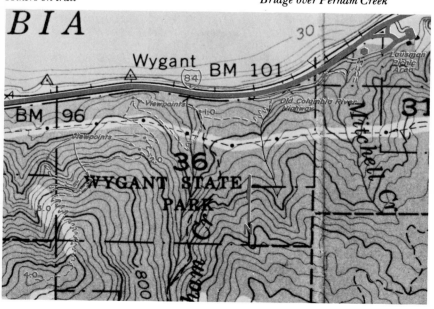

alphabetical index of trails

Cover photo: Multnomah Creek